# A Practical Guide to using Second Life in Higher Education

*Maggi Savin-Baden*

 Open University Press

Open University Press
McGraw-Hill Education
McGraw-Hill House
Shoppenhangers Road
Maidenhead
Berkshire
England
SL6 2QL

email: enquiries@openup.co.uk
world wide web: www.openup.co.uk

and Two Penn Plaza, New York, NY 10121-2289, USA

First published 2010

A catalogue record of this book is available from the British Library

ISBN-13: 978 0 335 24214 6
ISBN-10: 0 335 24214 6

Library of Congress Cataloging-in-Publication Data
CIP data has been applied for

Fictitous names of companies, products, people, characters and/or data that may be used herein (in case studies or in examples) are not intended to represent any real individual, company, product or event.

Typeset by Aptara Inc., India
Printed in the UK by CPI Antony Rowe, Chippenham and Eastbourne

For Anna, my beautiful and spirited daughter

# Contents

# Figures

# Tables

# Examples

# Acknowledgements

Immense thanks are due to the critical readers who took the time to correct, question and query this text before publication. I am indebted to Kate Boardman, David Burden, Michael Callaghan, Joff Chafer, Becca Khanna, Claire Major, Kerri McCusker, Christine Sinclair and Dave White.

Thanks are also due to those who have made contributions and supplied comments; these include all of the above as well as Kerry Cook, Fiona Littleton, Pramod Luthra, Hamish Macleod, Cathy Tombs and Ian Truelove.

Thanks, as ever, are also due to John Savin-Baden for his support, critique, proof reading and indexing.

The views expressed here and any errors are mine.

*Things change.*
*They always do, it's one of the things of nature. Most people are afraid*
*of change, but if you look at it as something you can always count on,*
*then it can be a comfort. There's not many things you can really count*
*on.*

(LaGravenese, 1995)

# Introduction

One damp, dark November night I arrived back from London, late for a dinner with the senior management of the university. As I hurtled into the room the vice chancellor asked me if I knew anything about Second Life, I nodded and sat down. By the end of the evening I had got the job of – and some funding for – setting up Coventry University Island. At the time I was still very much a 'newbie' and still see myself as an educational researcher rather than any kind of expert in virtual worlds. When Shona Mullen, Managing Director of Education at McGraw-Hill, asked me to take on this project it took some heart searching to decide if I could do it. My agreement to take on the writing of this book emerged out of my own difficulties of trying to develop effective teaching in Second Life, whilst being a student on an MSc in e-learning at the same time. So this is a book based not just on my experiences and ideas – both practical and pedagogical, but it has drawn on the expertise of those from around the world who are innovators, learning technologists and students, as well as those like me who have explored virtual worlds to see if they can help improve student learning and make teaching better. It is therefore a practical guide, based on educational theory which makes suggestions based on research and experience, but also seeks, in places, to help us to consider what learning in higher education is for, and how it might be possible to develop new technological uses for providing better learning.

Although there are currently a growing number of books about Second Life available, much of the focus has been on designing the environment, ways of building and the general ease and use-value of the environment. This book is aimed at those who want to use Second Life for teaching in further and higher education. It provides both an overview and an in-depth stance about aspects of the immersive world for teaching, learning and assessment, as well as suggestions about researching (in) Second Life.

Second Life is a 3D multi-user virtual world developed by Linden Lab in 2003, and is inhabited by millions of 'residents' across the world. In March 2010 a newer version <u>Viewer 2</u> was launched. Furthermore, it is used as a platform for education by many institutions, such as colleges, universities, libraries and government departments worldwide. The growth in the use of Second Life for learning and teaching in further and higher education since 2003 has promoted both excitement and concern. There have been many staff who have been delighted that such a medium can be used in higher education and that it is also one that prompts students to engage in learning with such enthusiasm and fun. Yet there have been others for whom the use of Second Life has been seen as problematic and prompted a deep sense of unease. Such unease has been confirmed by university management in some institutions by their refusal to allow the use of immersive virtual worlds for learning at all. This discomfort seems to be connected with questions about whether such spaces should be used for learning, and concerns about whether Second Life is only being used because it is seen as new and different, which in turn raises further questions about its relative value for learning. Further, the immersive nature of spaces such as Second Life also seems to prompt unease about the relationship between identities in real life and immersive worlds.

This book begins in Chapter 1 by exploring the value of using Second Life in higher education, why it has been adopted in higher education and then examines four possible reasons for its enduring use. Chapter 2 begins by suggesting that the most helpful way to begin using Second Life is for individuals or small groups to work with one another to design and develop Second Life use across their university. It recommends ways of supporting one another in the early stages and considers longer term issues such as gaining institutional support. The final section of the chapter offers an overview of other immersive virtual worlds that are available and might be adopted.

Chapter 3 explores the choices and decisions that need to be made when deciding how to plan, design and implement learning in Second Life and presents ideas and strategies for ensuring sound design. It suggests what works and what does not and offers guidance for designing effective scenarios and activities. Following this, Chapter 4 begins by exploring ways of reusing current practice such as lectures and seminars in Second Life and discusses the relative value of re-using such formats. The second section of the chapter suggests new ways of considering what learning might be in Second Life, suggesting which new media and different practices might be adopted.

In Chapter 5 it is argued that interactive and dialogic approaches are largely more useful than didactic ones in this environment. The chapter begins by examining some of the pedagogical challenges in using Second Life for learning and suggests the value of its use for higher education. It then explores the importance of identity, emotion and immersion for learning in Second Life. Chapters 6 and 7 develop from this, offer guidance on how to equip staff and support students in Second Life, and provide introductory activities and suggest ways of getting staff and students accustomed to learning in this environment. The literature on assessment of learning in Second Life is somewhat sparse. Chapter 8 suggests that the issue of assessment in Second Life does not differ from concerns about assessment in higher education in general; however it does explore this issue further and provides exemplars of assessment that fit effectively with the notion of assessment *for* learning in Second Life.

The final chapters of the book take a broader look at the technology and examine how Second Life can be used in conjunction with other media and suggest what the future might hold. Chapter 9 examines Second Life in the broader context of Web 2.0 technologies and new technological developments for enhancing learning. Some of these have been developed specifically for Second Life, whilst clearly others have not. Chapter 10 explores methodologies that are useful for research in immersive virtual worlds. It draws on research approaches that have been adapted for Second Life and also presents new and emerging methodologies. The final chapter, Chapter 11, considers emerging issues and begins by examining some of the new technologies on the horizon that might inform future learning genres. It suggests that areas such as proxemics, haptics and mobile technologies bear further exploration and recommends that augmented and mixed reality can offer much to distance learning.

This book provides pedagogically informed guidance and research-based suggestions for practice. It is not necessarily a text to read 'in one go' as it is divided into three parts. The idea is that those completely new to using Second Life for teaching begin with Part 1, but those wanting to develop their teaching begin with Part 2. For the experienced and the boundary crossers, Parts 2 or 3 are the place to start. Inevitably in a book such as this there will be numerous new terms; therefore I have explained many throughout the text, but a glossary is also provided. It is, however, not a book designed to provide all the answers, but to be something that provides guidance and suggestions, as well as tackling many of the questions and queries raised by those both enthusiastic and critical of using such spaces in higher education.

# Part 1

## Getting started in Second Life

# 1　The value of Second Life for learning in higher education

'So, what do you think of using Second Life then?' I asked

Steve: I love its openness, possibilities and the creativity it offers me as lecturer

Mike: Well I would like to bring it all together with Twitter, mobile technology and anything else to get platforms and systems to work together

Rachel: I just want us to share our ideas and build more, we need to share so we don't keep reinventing stuff

## Introduction

Perspectives on the use and value of Second Life in higher education vary considerably, but for those who have been using it for over three years its value, for most, is unquestionable. Despite some difficulties with it there are also many advantages, and although this book does not take an evangelistic stance, what it will do is explore the possibilities for Second Life use in higher education. This chapter begins by suggesting why it is that Second Life might be used in higher education and then examines four possible reasons for its enduring use. These are the value of Second Life as a visual approach to learning, the openness of it as a platform, the opportunity it brings for engaging with experiential learning, and finally the way it offers a mirror through which we can reflect on higher education practice.

## Why use immersive virtual worlds in higher education?

The advantage of using Second Life in higher education is that it is a space in which experimentation can occur in ways that are not possible in real life. For those in online and distance settings it offers an opportunity to develop communities, create trust and increase the sense of presence in learning. Yet it also provides a place to play with roles and identity, in that it offers an opportunity to undertake activities not normally physically possible, such as flying and changing identity. Further, activities under-taken in Second Life in general tend not to have real-life consequences – such as gender swapping or flying into buildings.

There have been many discussions about the uses and advantages of using Second Life (for example, Warburton, 2008, 2009) but it is perhaps more important to consider the particular values it might bring to a given course or module. Consider, for example, if it will facilitate learning at a distance, or will offer more flexibility for your students or programme. In some ways Second Life would seem to be an unusual platform (or world) to be adopted in higher education, but it is one that seems to have been embraced by many staff. Whilst it could be suggested that it has been adopted by some academics because they want to be subversive, most have adopted it because they wish to be innovative. For some staff it has been adopted because it is seen as an experimental and experiential space to use with students, because 'it is there', but I would suggest that the value of its use stretches beyond these kinds of motives.

Second Life was launched in 2003 by Linden Lab and despite media suggestions in 2010 it is neither dead, nor dying (as suggested by Corbyn, 2009), and probably has some considerable way to run before it is over-taken by something else. Indeed in March 2010 Viewer 2 was launched which increases the possibility for integration with other systems and software. There are other platforms that offer similar opportunities but it is Second Life that remains overwhelmingly the most popular. In many ways I would suggest Second Life introduces questions about pedagogy, practice and how learning might be improved and enhanced. It is still somewhat of a puzzle as to why Second Life has been taken up by higher education and I would suggest its relative enduring use is because of four main reasons:

- it provides a visual learning environment that is a creative learning space
- its very openness interrupts not only teaching and learning prac-tices but also issues of power and control in learning
- it offers experiential learning opportunities, chiefly in terms of us-ing simulations, demonstrations and experiences not always avail-able in real life, particularly in education for the professions
- it serves as a mirror to higher education practice across different levels.

## The value of the visual

Higher education has moved from blackboard and chalk, through over-head projectors and flip charts on to PowerPoint, and this, together with society's increasing use of television and computer games, has resulted in a culture that increasingly focuses on the visual. Accounts from staff and students would seem to indicate that many university students use social networking (such as Twitter and Facebook) rather than communicate via the university virtual learning environment. Although this does not account for the use of Second Life, what it does shed light on is the value of social networking for learning, something which higher education should perhaps capitalise on more than it currently does so.

While the (often) ordered university virtual learning environments still continue (such as Blackboard), and indeed were considered innovative in their day, immersive platforms such as Second Life offer a visual experience, and a sense of 'being' in a learning space in ways that managed learning systems do not. Even if this very visuality may not be vital for students on face-to-face courses; it does appear to help those on distance programmes to feel more engaged with peers and what is being learned on the course. Whether it is learning to build, finding new clothes or learning through discussion, Second Life also seems to help students to build a learning community. Perhaps this is due to the fact that Second Life is a synchronous learning space and therefore its immediacy brings with it a perspective of being and learning with others in a way that other asynchronous forms of learning do not.

The value of the visual nature of Second Life is in the ability to use it for learning in visual ways not possible in real life. For example, it is possible to build houses that replicate real life homes in which occupational therapists can evaluate whether the house is suitable for a patient to return to following a hip replacement. It is possible to create a crime scene where police students can consider how to take photographs and understand the importance of not contaminating it. For paramedic students it is possible to engage with an accident and gain feedback on their performance without the risk of someone dying through their mistakes. These exemplars might seem little more than basic simulation, but they are ones that staff and students themselves can design and build – with the help of a learning technologist, and then adapt over time. It is a world that allows you to choose how you look and what you wear, so that you also possess both an inventory that contains everything that your avatar 'owns' and an expandable set of 'gestures' that allow an individual to animate their avatar's movements. Second Life then offers a means of practising and exploring skills in a visual environment which would not be available in real life, but for many staff it is also seen as an approach that fits with the pedagogy of their discipline. Disciplines shape the nature of pedagogy and such pedagogies reflect the practices and culture of the discipline. Yet it is not just the visual nature of Second Life that is appealing, it is also the openness it offers.

## The value of openness

Second Life is an environment that can be used freely and as aforementioned, it is not necessary for staff or students to pay to join or to buy land. The ability just to use an interesting space, to provide learning as a visual environment is appealing. This is because it brings a sense of freedom from the often bounded university systems and restrictions. In Second Life it is not necessary to book a room and it is relatively easy to find or create space not normally used for teaching, such as a wild space or a beach. It seems that its very openness and flexibility is something that staff not only value for teaching but also use for socialising, and for some even 'being' in Second Life on a beach, while writing a troublesome report, is seen as beneficial. This openness too seems to bring with it a sense of freedom to think differently about teaching and learning but it also offers opportunities to try out new and different activities. Staff often speak of it as a space that is more like the bar; it is a social medium where informality, ingenuity and wit are valued. However, there is also recognition that such openness brings challenges so that Second Life is seen as an open but somewhat divided culture where the creative and the materialistic sides of the space could be seen to vie with one another. It is a creative and experimental space and in many ways might be seen as a 'third space'. The notion of the 'third space' captures the idea that there are 'particular discursive spaces . . . in which alternative and competing discourses and positioning transform conflict and difference into rich zones of collaboration and learning' (Gutiérrez et al., 1999: 286–7). Second Life is such a discursive space, a space in which building, changing spaces, experimenting and learning differently creates a polycontextual space, which for some staff will offer a move away from performativity. An example of a teaching approach where such openness is explicit and encouraged is when staff and students worked to learn how to learn and build together in Second Life as Dave White, University of Oxford explains below:

> As part of the JISC funded Open Habitat project we piloted the use of Second Life with art and design undergraduates based at Leeds Metropolitan University and online distance philosophy students based out of the University of Oxford. While the art and design students met face-to-face for the initial part of the pilots, for much of the time they were logged into SL from home. Initially around 150 art and design students were put through a 1 hour workshop in OpenSim (an open source version of SL) to give them a sense of the software. This allowed us to give each student their

own island and separated the social pressures associated with a multi-user virtual world from the pragmatic need to get to grips with the software. In a previous run of the pilot we had discovered that despite the sense of co-presence in world it was difficult for students to collaborate closely on design and building projects. This is partially to do with the way object permissions work in SL, but it was also a mis-interpretation of the pedagogy of the course. In art and design it is unusual for students to collaborate on the production of an artefact. The traditional RL 'design studio' space is laid out with personal working areas but in such a way that students can see each other practise. Discussion or inspiration might arise from this approach as work is highly visible.

In an attempt to align our approach in SL to this 'design studio' principle the activities in the next pilot were created so that students were part of a shared endeavour but could each bring their own interpretations to it. The first example of this was one in which the students played a word association game inworld for a few minutes then chose their favourite 'moment' from the game. An extension of this form of shared (but not strictly collaborative) activity was what became known as the tree building day. Students were asked to build a tree in one of a number of thematic styles (an evil tree, a love tree). The group went to an empty island and spent a few hours building their chosen trees alongside each other. Significantly the tutor also undertook the task and in doing so became a 'more experienced other' rather than an authority figure. In keeping with the virtual design studio idea, the students could see each others' practice emerging and could discuss approaches and techniques. They could also see the tutor's practice and ask for help and advice when necessary.

Overall the piloting moved from a focus on role based collaboration to a point at which individual practice could be developed in a studio style context. Ultimately much of the collaboration came through communication rather than shared practice in the creation of design artefacts. This, I feel, both reflected the pedagogy of the course and took advantage of the co-presence aspects of SL.

This kind of openness to learning and teaching largely reflects transformational theories of learning whereby learning shapes people in such a profound way that it affects all subsequent learning (Mezirow, 1981; Freire, 1972, 1974), as well as dialogic learning. Yet it is also a space that seems to

**Figure 1.1** Picture of tree building session (reproduced with permission)

encourage the use of dialogic learning. Dialogic learning (Mezirow, 1985) is a form of learning where students draw upon their own experience to explain the concepts and ideas with which they are presented, and then use that experience to make sense for themselves and also to explore further issues. Dialogue brings to the fore, for students and tutors, the value of prior experience to current learning and thus can engage them in explorations of and (re)constructions of their beliefs about learning. Such transformational and dialogic approaches also overlap into forms of experiential learning, which are valued approaches to teaching in Second Life.

## The value of experiential opportunities

For many staff the initial rationale for using Second Life in higher education is because practising skills within a virtual environment online offers advantages over learning through real-life practice, in particular the exposure of learners to a wide range of scenarios (more than they are likely to meet in a standard face-to-face programme) at a time and pace convenient to the learner, together with consistent feedback. Such experiential practices are increasingly seen as important when the opportunity to try out learning and explore practice are increasingly limited for students being educated for the professions. It also offers learners the chance to make mistakes without real-world repercussions. As Richter (2007) has argued:

> Therapists, soldiers, pilots, lawyers, business people, doctors, nurses, and teachers all normally engage in real life role play while learning the contexts and conditions particular to their professions during their days at the university or in training. Multi-User Virtual Environments (MUVEs) like Second Life are uniquely suited media for developing role playing scenarios to engage learning, if we provide the right mix of opportunity and structure. Indeed, role playing in Second Life and other MUVEs may represent perhaps one of the single most compelling educational opportunities for adults in the 21st Century.
>
> (Richter, 2007)

Although experiential learning was an approach to learning largely popularised in the 1980s it has since become subsumed into many teaching approaches and activities. Yet it is to this approach to learning that the use of Second Life can be most effectively linked. Weil and McGill (1989) developed the idea of four villages of experiential learning:

*Village 1* The assessment and accreditation of prior experiential learning – here experiential learning is about valuing, recording and assessing experience.

*Village 2* Experiential learning and change in higher and continuing education – here Weil and McGill draw on the work of Dewey (1938), suggesting that this form of experiential learning centres on exploring prior learning through reflection on life experience.

*Village 3* Experiential learning and social change – in this village there is a sense of learners being encouraged to move beyond their personal stance, and examine the broader sociocultural contexts and the impact these have on shaping not only their world but also their reflections on it.

*Village 4* Personal growth and development – here learners are encouraged to focus on growth and development through personal reflection and through communication and inter-relationships with others.

Experiential learning has been defined in a number of ways, but perhaps the most helpful is that of Saddington (1998: 134), who argues for three overarching perspectives which he then uses as lenses to locate the wider literature. These perspectives are:

- Progressive, whereby education is seen as a problem-solving instrument of social and political reform and the focus is therefore on responsibility towards society
- Humanist, which sees the learner at the centre of a process of growth and becoming
- Radical, which encourages learners to question the cultural assumptions of experience and move toward transformation.

Saddington tabulated these to summarise the main theoretical perspectives, seen in Table 1.1:

**Table 1.1**    Theoretical tradition of experiential learning

|  | *Progressive* | *Humanist* | *Radical* |
|---|---|---|---|
| Social problem taken most seriously | Social change | Personal meaningfulness | Oppression |
| Underlying theory of social development | Reform | Self-actualisation | Social transformation |
| Best metaphor for educational practice | Problem solving | Personal growth | Empowerment |
| Key value | Democracy | Acceptance | Freedom |
| What counts as 'knowledge'? | Judgement and the ability to act | Wholeness | Praxis (reflective thought and action) |
| The educators' task | Guiding | Support | Conscientisation |
| How an educated person is described | Responsible | Integrated | Liberated |
| Role of learner's life experience | A source of learning and inseparable from knowledge | The source of knowledge and the content of curriculum | Back to understanding socialite contexts and the source of knowledge |
| The type of experience mainly used | Structured | Personal focus | Self in society |
| Villages at work | 1 and 2 | 1 and 4 | 3 |

Many staff adopting Second Life would probably suggest that they are at the more radical end of the spectrum, because of the creative opportunities and the means of interrupting current pedagogic practice that it offers.

With the increasing use of distance programmes, Second Life creates online learning opportunities which are sufficiently immersive and collaborative outside the tutorial room, in ways that some managed learning systems do not. However, what is also important to note is the way in which Second Life enables learners not only to relate strongly to real life experiences but also to focus on the importance of learning *with* and *through* experience. Dewey (1938) emphasised the human capacity to reconstruct experience and thus make meaning of it, and suggested that education should be seen as a process of continuous reconstruction and growth of experience. He believed that the role of the teacher was to organise learning activities which built on the previous experiences of the students, and direct them to new experiences that furthered their growth. Thus the curriculum should be closely tied to the students' experiences, developmentally appropriate and structured in ways that fostered continuity. Dewey opposed theories of knowledge that considered knowledge specialised and independent of its role in problem-solving inquiry. Second Life, as Dewey (1938) would have argued, should be seen not as marked by the opposition between the idea that education is something which is developed from within *or* from without, but as something that seeks to embrace the ideal of a multifaceted learner with diverse experience, both internal, informal and social as well as external, formal and individual, with an acknowledgment that interaction of the various components of the learner's identities and experiences necessarily affect one another.

In terms of Second Life, experiential learning, of whatever type, comes into its own through the synchronicity of learning which bring questions about the nature and purpose of higher education.

## The value of Second Life as a mirror on higher education practices

The use of Second Life in higher education has created a stir in some quarters for a whole raft of reasons – mostly around purpose, pedagogy and pornography. However, such questioning has then prompted further queries being raised about teaching and learning in general. For example, concerns about the use of Second Life has resulted in questions being asked about why subjects are taught in particular ways, how teaching can be adapted and how learning can be improved. The introduction of Second Life has also raised questions about the institutional power and control of learning. This might be reflected in who controls the university island or what is allowed or disallowed in that space, as well as what is and is not acceptable practice. Many people have asked all sorts of questions about why we might want to learn in such a space and whether learning through an avatar is really any better than learning through discussion boards. Developing learning in Second Life therefore introduces a challenge about how we design curricula, and how we can design them for more process-based approaches to learning, and in particular social learning. In short it holds up a mirror to current pedagogies and practices in higher education and helps us to consider why and how we do what we do.

It is also important to recognise that there are still relatively few experiences worldwide about what does and does not work effectively in Second Life. Whilst evidence is mounting and much of what is discussed is shared practice, relatively few new pedagogical models have emerged and theorisation is only just beginning. It is important to consider, therefore, the relationship between the use of Second Life and the subject or discipline in which it is being used. There has been increasing discussion about discipline-based pedagogy worldwide (Jenkins and Zetter, 2003). Thus in discussion about the use of Second Life within the curriculum, it is important to consider the way in which disciplines themselves shape the teaching practices and belief systems. For example, teacher knowledge and beliefs about what to do, how to do it and under which circumstances, can affect the way that students learn a particular subject matter. Furthermore, it is also important to recognise that what works well and effectively the first time may not do so subsequently, and vice versa. Perhaps what is also important then when deciding to use Second Life is to differentiate between reasons for adopting Second Life, such as activities that cannot be done in real life, and reasons for using it instead of something else, for example instead of a discussion forum.

Approaches to teaching in Second Life differ not only because of the medium being used but also because of the nature of immersion that occurs in that environment. This is because 'being' in Second Life prompts us and our students to engage with issues of embodiment and questions about positioning and power. For example, some questions that relate to these issues might include staff asking does it matter if:

- Students come to class as an animal or naked?
- Students stand, dance or walk off in the middle of a discussion?
- Students come to class carrying a gun?
- Students change their clothes while the teacher is speaking?

Whilst at one level these questions might seem obvious and simplistic, they do raise questions about what learning might or should look like. It introduces questions about the role of staff and students in such spaces and issues relating to levels of engagement, real world behaviours and issues of space in these immersive environments. A number of authors describe presence as the sense of being 'in' or 'part of' a 3D virtual world. Thus the sense of presence in Second Life means not only feeling 'there' with other staff and students and guided to learn, but also feeling as if they are actually present in that environment (Beer et al., 2003). This absorption and engagement of the student in the learning experience is argued to focus and improve learning (Kang et al., 2008; Richardson and Newby, 2006). Further, Dede (1995) suggests that within learning environments, immersion can be created through the capacity to execute actions, through semantics and semiotics, and through physical and sensory provision that creates a feeling that the user is surrounded by the 3D virtual world. The inclusion and exploration of emotion, embodiment and presence in learning, however, would seem somewhat of a departure for higher education. Yet although, as I have suggested, there are a number of reasons why staff have adopted Second Life over other virtual worlds, it does seems that the capacity to create, customise and build with relative ease remains a strong draw. At the same time the possibilities Second Life offers for linking with other websites and maximising the possibility for integrating different forms of knowledge and communication within and across disciplines, platforms and time zones are seen as extremely beneficial.

## Conclusion

This chapter has explored the value of Second Life to higher education and suggested some reasons for the growth and maintenance of its use. Yet it is important that universities adopt strategies that enable them to use this space in ways that not only challenge issues around power and pedagogy, but also that they understand how this might be possible. Many staff and students take on learning and teaching in Second Life without realising the possible mistakes it is easy to make, and the consequences of some of the assumptions they bring to working in this world. Practical steps to island development, ensuring the support of senior management and effective planning can help this process and it is to this we turn in Chapter 2.

# 2 Practical tips for getting started

'Don't build a seat on a slope – it tips over'

## Introduction

Having explored some of the values of using Second Life in higher education this chapter will offer practical guidance on how to implement Second Life. It begins by suggesting the most helpful way is for individuals or small groups to work with one another to design and develop its use across the university. It recommends ways of supporting one another in the early stages and considers longer terms issues such as gaining and maintaining institutional support to provide financial assistance as well as island development and management. The final section of the chapter offers an overview of other immersive virtual worlds that are available and might also be adopted.

## Getting started

Second Life is a 'world' with its own financial system complete with a currency and the ability to trade goods and services. It has a navigation/map system for travelling around and a 'search' system for finding people and places, like shops. Whilst it is free for individuals to use, to adopt it for university teaching requires the purchase of land, but the costs are relatively small and this is reflected in the increasing use of Second Life across the higher education sector worldwide. However, strictly speaking universities do not have to buy land, but may ask permission to borrow space from other universities. It is also possible to teach in open areas such as the mainland as well as using space such as the Sistine chapel on Vassar Island and Ancient Rome as places of exploration for students. Alternatively you can avoid Second Life's usually hectic orientation areas and enter Second Life directly at New Media Consortium (NMC) NMC Orientation island. To do that you will need to create your Second Life account at the NMC's website instead of at the Second Life site.

Inevitably in any kind of innovation, staff have mixed reactions. This section is concerned with ways of building a strong and vibrant Second Life community both within and across higher education institutions.

### Find Second Life innovators across the university

As with any innovation, it is important to find a critical mass of innovators and early adopters, who are enthusiastic and can begin development. Whilst there are many theories of innovation and sustainability, in the original adoption and diffusion model Rogers (1962) argued that people tend to respond to innovation in five particular ways. In relation to implementing Second Life they might be seen as follows:

1) *Innovators, the enthusiasts* pursue both the idea and the implementation of Second Life and it is often their latest obsession.
2) *Early adopters, the visionaries* are like innovators in that they get involved in a project such as Second Life early on, once the decision to implement it has been made. They find it easy to imagine the benefits of the approach.
3) *Early majority, the pragmatists* share some of the early adopters' ability to see the benefits of the approach, but they are practical, aware of the dangers of passing fads and so are content to wait to see if it is likely to be successful, before they commit themselves to this approach.
4) *Late majority, the conservatives* share the same concerns as the early majority. They are not comfortable with the introduction of new approaches and so they will wait until it has become an established mode of practice.
5) *Laggards, the sceptics* do not want anything to do with this new approach and may even try to sabotage it at any stage of its implementation.

Even if funding to support Second Life introduction is supplied by senior management, ensuring that the innovation is guided by lecturing staff and supported by learning technologists is vital. However, it is also important that staff receive support and guidance from experts, and can use each other for mutual support. Providing space for discussion and mentoring in the early stages is important. Fiona Littleton, University of Edinburgh remarked: 'the best learning experiences are those that surprise you, like working with tutors new to Second Life and watching their attitude towards it change and seeing them become part of a community'. The suggestions which follow may help to move toward the building of a community in your institution.

### Organise lunchtime sessions

These can be short and fluid, allowing staff to just attend for 20 minutes if that is all the time they have. Examples of sessions that seem to work well are:

- 'Open house' show and tell demonstration in lecture theatres to prompt debates and enable staff to ask questions. By inviting key personnel who you think may be interested as well as others who may be cynical, is a helpful way to prompt debate. Showing Machinima or getting colleagues to be inworld to demonstrate Second Life are all useful activities that can help staff to understand what using this technology might mean in their own teaching arenas.
- Demonstrations in real life of inworld activities. One of the sessions I ran with colleagues in early 2006 was a session in a large lecture theatre to demonstrate the newly contracted university island. Having had initial discussions with key staff, this next session was open to the whole university. I had asked staff what and if they wanted anything built on their particular space (we had split the island into an archipelago to prevent academic arguments about space) on the island. Most people did not really know. In my enthusiasm I found a castle which I put on the Maths island, but during the presentation the Professor of Maths was somewhat displeased with a castle with huge battlements being put in his space – because he saw it as part of a larger metaphor of maths as a learning barrier. I thought he made a very fair point, but if I had not put the castle there in the first place discussion of symbolism and proxemics may not have been raised until much later in the island's development.
- Provide sandbox sessions in computer labs for staff to come and explore and receive some mentoring. A sandbox session is where staff meet in Second Life in an area designated for building (a sandbox) and the idea is that it is a space of experimentation and discussion where people help one another.
- Provide building tutorials for those interested. Often although the focus is on building, the interaction and discussion between staff tends to focus on wider issues about teaching in Second Life.

### Set up a co-mentoring scheme

A cross university support group or mentoring scheme can offer staff an opportunity to share achievements and failures – face to face or at inworld meetings. This kind of scheme can be undertaken both within and across the university. For example, an informal scheme can be used where staff interested in developing a Second Life module can be mentored by some-one more experienced. An alternative option is to create national support through a face-to-face workshop where ideas and practices can be shared, but which has plenty of space for networking and informal discussion. For example, <u>The National Workshop on Learning in Immersive Virtual Worlds</u>, which has links, presentations, and filmed sessions (and when it occurs it is also streamed inworld). There are many other events publicised through the <u>Second Life Educators</u> mailing lists, <u>Second Life Research Listserv</u> inworld building workshops, and in the UK, activities and forums provided by the <u>JISC Regional Support Centres</u>.

### Create a flying squad to support staff

The difficulty of developing and maintaining the island as well as rede-veloping it annually to ensure that it meets the needs of the university, is often seen as a barrier to development. However, by using a student 'flying squad' it is possible to provide support for staff, keep up with Second Life developments in general and manage the updates and changes required. The flying squad scheme can be managed by a project officer with expe-rience in Second Life. The flying squad itself comprises students who are trained by the project officer in building, scripting and guiding staff on ways of using Second Life for teaching – and are paid by the hour. In prac-tice, members of staff who want help with building or to gain guidance on how to use Second Life for teaching, contact the project officer who ascertains their requirements and then allocates a flying squad member to the task. A proforma (Table 2.1) can be used to help with this, which enables the member of staff to try to work out what their requirements are before they meet with the project officer. Support can also be provided from within the Learning Innovation Unit, Coventry University, for any-one wanting particular help with pedagogical design for Second Life.

**Table 2.1** Proforma for staff requirements

Staff name, email and phone number
Discipline
Module in which Second Life is to be used
Short description of module
Experience of Second Life to date
Support required:
   1) Introduction to Second Life
   2) Development of ideas
   3) Providing building
   4) Guidance on teaching

Whether you are a member of staff wanting to develop Second Life in a module or someone in academic development or the e-learning unit, planning and design is essential at the outset of development.

# Gaining support from senior management

This seems to be very varied across the sector. Some universities are not allowed to use Second Life at all, others have free access and others have restrictions imposed with very clear parameters. The freedom to use Second Life across the university with a download option through the university system is the best approach. The only real danger is in loss of Intellectual Property with staff leaving the institution, but this can be dealt with by having clear guidance relating to permission.

### Strategies for gaining and maintaining support

#### *Provide a strategy*

In order to initially develop and then critically sustain the use of Second Life in your university, it is important to provide university management with a 3–4 year plan and an immediate implementation strategy. The immediate plan should focus on bringing together interested parties from across the university and providing support for development in terms of guidance and seed funding. The long term strategy should focus on sustainability. An example of an initial proposal that may be submitted to the university senior management team is provided in Figure 2.1 opposite:

The long term strategy should focus on ways to sustain and develop activities both within university departments and also across the university as a whole. This should include:

1) The use of Second Life in institutional teaching, learning, research and e-learning strategies
2) Technological support
    - Ensure easy access to Second Life on university homepage
    - Meetings between ICT departments and academics about requirements and understandings of both parties
    - Development of ethics guidelines
3) Gain development funding: internal and external
4) Staff development
5) Provision of guidelines and suggestions for use
6) Development of opportunities for sharing practices
7) Dissemination of good practice within and beyond the university

**Introduction and Background**

This proposal covers a suggested development strategy for the Second Life Virtual Island being leased over three years by this University. It follows an initial exploratory meeting between interested parties. It is important to recognise the accelerating trends in education away from traditional lecture-based approaches towards peer-to-peer, personalised and collaborative learning environments. It could be very strategically important, therefore, for the University to provide these tools and technologies as part of the learning mix, not only to continuously develop the effectiveness of its programmes, but also to attract, engage and retain future students. The University virtual island can provide an opportunity to achieve a number of aims:

- To provide a rich and creative technology platform around which to develop a variety of applications
- To build the University's capacity for the development and exploitation of 3D virtual worlds
- To raise the profile of the University as a potential leader in this sector
- To facilitate cross-disciplinary collaboration between artists, scientists and technologists
- To provide new pedagogic opportunities to engage with Web 2.0 technologies
- To develop excellence in research and gain external educational funding for research into Web 2.0 technologies
- To engage new partners within industry and the arts
- To support the local strategic development
- This proposal seeks to put forward a multi-faceted approach to the development of the island, the resources needed, and the potential funding opportunities for further development.

**Suggested development approach**

Second Life provides a set of proprietary tools to create buildings and objects and also to develop scripts to control the behaviour of those objects. Whilst these tools can be used by people with a wide range of abilities, effective development of a space within SL does require a strategic approach and some support both from a technical and creative perspective as well as the provision of online, inworld mentoring. The suggested development approach, working with the interested parties identified thus far is to:

- Plan a layout for the island based on a central hub with support services linked to individual projects identified at the initial meeting
- Undertake an impact analysis for disabled students
- Use experts such as SL consultants and local champions within the University to 'fast-track' the development
- Set up a researcher to support both funding bids and individual developments
- Employ a good technician with both design and coding skills to support the development of end-user capacity for design and coding
- Use the services of an online moderator to act as a resident guide and mentor to visitor/users

**Possible application areas for the university**

The following potential application areas have already been identified and each could be represented by a building area within Second Life:

- A virtual performing arts centre for learning applications and virtual performances
- A virtual Students Union developed by the students
- Problem based learning Master's degree module in SL
- A virtual mathematics centre addressing some existing training needs
- A virtual business idea competition based around SL enterprise
- Research into SL and disability based around an existing disabled entrepreneur using SL

Champions in different disciplines will work to expand these ideas and seek out funding to support the projects

**Initial start-up plan**

Building on the initial interest, the project might develop using the following components:

- SL workshop and demonstration arranged and co-ordinated by key members of staff
- Development of funding bids and identification of potential partners
- Set up of steering group and working parties
- Promotion campaign to identify and recruit local champions
- Planning and development workshops supported by expert developers
- Recruitment and appointment of research, technical and mentoring staff
- Regular meetings for progress monitoring and sharing of ideas
- Set up of community of interest, blog, wiki and e-newsletter

**Figure 2.1** Second Life development proposal

A three-year plan could be as follows (see Table 2.2):

**Table 2.2**   Three-year implementation plan

---

### Year 1 Pre-implementation period
1) Exploration of relevant literature
2) Meetings between ICT departments and academics about requirements and understandings of both parties
3) Speaking with those who have implemented SL already in their university
4) Inworld and real world meetings with current technical and academic experts in this field
5) Discussion with course leaders and deans about needs and possibilities
6) Discussion with external stakeholders
7) Evaluate course materials and activities being used in other universities and via literature.

Develop start-up plan:
- Promotion campaign to identify and recruit local champions
- SL workshop and demonstration arranged and co-ordinated by key members of staff
- Regular meetings for progress monitoring and sharing of ideas
- Set up of community of interest: blog, wiki and e-newsletter
- Set up of steering group and working parties
- Planning and development workshops supported by expert developers.

### Year 2: Implementation
1) Plan a layout for the island based on a central hub with support services linked to individual projects identified at the initial meeting
2) Use experts and local champions within the university to 'fast-track' the development
3) Appoint or locate a researcher to support both funding bids and individual developments
4) Employ a technician with both design and coding skills to support the development of end-user capacity for design and coding
5) Locate an online moderator to act as a resident guide and mentor to visitor/users
6) Provision of guidelines and suggestions for use across the university. For example:
    - The development of SL materials should involve all groups of staff contributing to the delivery of a particular module
    - The production of learning resources is vital to the success of SL, and related departments need to be involved from the outset
7) Develop ethics guidelines
8) Develop risk management strategy: this could will include a risk log with appropriate management steps and designated risk owner who has the responsibility to monitor that risk over the course of the development
9) Development of 'flying squad' (see below)
10) Implement iterative evaluation process.

---

*(continued)*

**Table 2.2**   Three-year implementation plan (*Continued*)

**Year 3–4**

1) Recruitment and appointment of long term research, technical and mentoring staff to sustain development
2) Development of funding bids and identification of potential partners
3) Develop reusable objects and tools that can be adopted and adapted across courses
4) Develop university repository for materials and objects
5) Creation of database of national and international experts
6) An annual workshop or conference

## Buying islands

This involves the university buying space and then paying a monthly rental. This offers privacy and security in terms of building and teaching – although unless the island is kept as a constantly secure space this can mean you may have people wandering into seminars. Buying an island can be complex as the island will be 'attached' to a single avatar, which might be a member of staff who subsequently leaves the institution. Thus it is best for it to be attached to someone senior in the organisation. However, technically you do not need to own land unless you either want to build your own environment or you want to meet privately. If you do want to use some land then there are many educational organisations from which you can rent land.

## Using external support

There are a number of ways of gaining external support and in particular building support. These are advertised via blogs, the Second Life Educators list and through Second Life itself. Reliable companies in the UK include Daden and CitrusVirtual who understand the practices and parameters of Higher Education and offer a sound and conscientious service; and other solution providers in Second Life can be found via the Second Life website. What is important to remember about using external support is that the company needs to support your institution's higher education values. For example, linking with a company who wants to work with a university to develop products may bring advantages in terms of recurrent funding, but it may prevent the development of open source ware. Thus if reusability and open source principles are central to the development you are undertaking, it is perhaps more important to work with a company who not only has expertise in this area, but also who shares your appreciation of interoperability and the importance of open standards.

## Development of space

The development of Second Life and deciding who should pay for development can be controversial. This section presents some possible solutions.

### Costs

The cost of renting and maintaining an island is relatively inexpensive; what is more demanding is the initial design and set up of your island. Table 2.3 provides an illustration of funding a developing scheme for institutional development over the first year of a project.

### Privacy

It is possible to keep other people out of your island by configuring it for geographical privacy. This means that access to an island is restricted and that others will not be able to teleport in. Whoever owns the island at your university can set privacy options from the Estate tab and can request the island to be locked down at given times for teaching if preferred. Thus it is possible to restrict access so only people on the allowed residents and allowed groups lists can gain access to the island. It is also possible to create property lines within your island; more information about this is provided here.

### Allocation of island space

Coventry University Island is, at present divided into a number of distinct areas. There is a main central area, which primarily acts as an introduction and information hub to the island as a whole, with recognisable real life spaces such as The Alan Berry Building (see Figure 2.2) and Lanchester Library.

The island also has spaces to display a mixture of real world and inworld designs such as gallery and shop spaces. Around the central island are a number of smaller island spaces each of which can be run independently by its own management team. These can cater for a specific area of interest such as: problem-based learning, maths, performance, serious games and business. Above the island there are a number of sandboxes; spaces dedicated to the exploration of inworld design and creation, where anyone is able to experiment and build. Much of the teaching for building and scripting takes place in an extensive sandbox above the island where students can leave their work for a period of weeks. Some universities have chosen not to divide their island into disciplinary hubs but

**Table 2.3** Funding scheme for institutional development of Second Life

| Proposal | Activity | Cost |
| --- | --- | --- |
| Run five SL workshops open to all staff | Introductory workshops x 3: Teaching and Learning in SL Advanced workshops x 2: User-led | Indirect cost (2 staff and students to run) |
| Continue to employ second year/post grad students to work as 'flying squad' to build in Second Life and work with staff | 4 Students £7 per hour for 36 weeks (approx 4 hours per week) | £4,032 |
| Fund member of staff 3 hours a week | 1) Manage flying squad with staff lead 2) Co-lead workshops with staff lead 3) Manage island 4) Liaise with staff re building and maintenance of island 5) Develop new projects | £4,000 |
| Employ external consultant | To run 2 further training days for staff and to support staff | £1,500 |
| Employ greeter | To meet those arriving on the island 3 hours a day 180 days $500 Linden dollars per hour | £600 |
| Special project fund | To buy out staff/students for unplanned building and support projects over year | £600 |
| Events fund | For presenting, publicity and conference events over the year | £500 |
| Dedicated SL computer | For student team and greeter | £700 (Including VAT) |
| Total | | £11,932 |

have encouraged staff to share buildings and space in order to maximise cross-disciplinary collaboration.

Second Life is an important and vital learning space since learning in late modernity, particularly in virtual worlds, offers little space for stability, since knowledge and learning always appear to be on the move. Thus, it is questionable as to whether one can have any kind of stability

**Figure 2.2** Coventry University: The Alan Berry Building in Second Life

in higher education now and in the future. Second Life spaces are not only transient spaces, but also spaces where it is possible to see that what one once believed to be truths and ways of being are now merely contingent and provisional. Developing learning in Second Life therefore introduces a challenge about how we design curricula for more process-based approaches to learning and in particular social learning. Perhaps it is time to move away from outcomes, objectives and competencies, towards intentions, understanding and student-guided designs.

## The problem of the 'always empty' feeling

One of the comments many people make about Second Life is that of arriving on an island where nobody is present. One of the ways around this is to provide either a chatbot or a greeter. A chatbot is a character not controlled by a user within Second Life, but who has been programmed for specific purposes. The chatbot can be commanded to do certain actions such as moving around, pointing out areas to explore and information displays, and answering basic questions. The other option is to pay a 'greeter' who is alerted when someone arrives on the island and will then show visitors around and answer questions. By using 2 3 greeters from different time zones it is then possible to have someone in the space for 24 hours a day. Nevertheless unless you are providing a considerable number of international distance learning programmes that use Second Life this is probably not a requirement for most universities. Using a greeter is relatively inexpensive and they are usually paid around £6 an hour. There are also volunteer greeters and more information related to this can be found on the Second Life Wiki. However, there remain some discussions about the status of greeters and some are classed as part-time employees.

### Staff engagement

There are a number of models for supporting staff new to Second Life. The most common ones are to use a mentoring system for building islands and infrastructure, or a co-facilitating scheme to assist teaching. A scheme developed at Coventry University was a Second Life Flying Squad (see page 21 for more details). However, some staff see Second Life as just a game that should not be used for learning. Certainly many comments in the press have not helped this perception. It is vital to introduce staff to effective and well supported educational projects in Second Life in order to help them to see the possibilities, and this is discussed in more detail in Chapter 6.

## Learning in different worlds

Although currently Second Life would seem to be the immersive virtual world adopted most in higher education, there are other options available. Generally, a user interacts with people, objects and places in these virtual worlds using an avatar. An avatar is a virtual presence which may or may not be representative of a user's real life identity. An avatar will have a name, and in most instances (though not necessarily all) a distinct visual appearance. There are a number of virtual worlds in operation, which all take very different approaches to creating 'realities'. For example, some are photo-realistic, others impressionistic, some focus on fantasy, others reality but most have an emphasis on the interaction. Yet currently it would seem that few implementing learning within immersive virtual worlds consider the practices adopted and their relationship with pedagogy. It seems as if ideas are just implemented and tried out with little reference to the literature, or consideration of how previous literature and practice might or might not inform what they plan and implement. The questions raised here are not entirely answered in this chapter but it is important to consider which pedagogical approaches fit with which technologies, and what new approaches and practices are needed. This chapter explores some of the issues related to such a question.

Understanding how virtual worlds relate to each other and how their differences cause them to have different pedagogical value is important.

## OpenSim

The open source version of Second Life is OpenSim. It is a 3D Application Server used to create a virtual world and may be accessed through a variety of clients, on multiple protocols. It can be installed and run locally and is under constant development in an attempt to bring it in line with the level of functionality of Second Life. This does require some technical support and know-how but these skills should be well within the remit of your IT/computing department. There are many who still suggest it does demand considerable time and energy to set up. Yet the advantage of OpenSim is that the age restriction of Second Life is removed and this will therefore be useful for universities working across higher and further education. It is worth remembering though that OpenSim will not have a large 'community' of avatars within it and so some of the social and resource aspects of Second Life will be lost. Given OpenSim is a closed environment and therefore students will not encounter unusual others and griefers it might be seen as something that will reduce the interest and challenge of being in Second Life. For many staff the interruptions, encounters and challenges with different avatars are seen as an important part of the learning experience and therefore to use OpenSim would remove this.

## Project Wonderland

This was originally funded by Sun/Oracle, but is now attempting to become an independent venture, Wonderland is a virtual world that was primarily developed for business teams to work together across the globe. The initial idea for its use stemmed from 'on-boarding' – the desire to get new staff on board with the company. It is open source but requires considerable work to build from scratch, using JavaScript. This is in fact an open source toolkit for creating collaborative 3D virtual worlds. It can be built specifically for an institution but the graphics are not as clear as Second Life, the initial building is time consuming and costly and avatar customisation is very limited. An example of this is Mirtle, funded by Sun Education. This is a mixed reality teaching and learning environment, which has sought to investigate the use of mixed reality virtual worlds to bring together virtual students with live classroom lectures using the virtual world toolkit Project Wonderland.

## ActiveWorlds

This is very similar to Second Life although it was developed beforehand and it was based on the idea of being a 3D-equivalent of a 2D web browser.

ActiveWorlds started as WebWorld in 1994 and became ActiveWorlds in 1995 but then the company experienced difficulties. In 2006 the public world server version 4.1 was released. However, it has never really gained the same popularity as Second Life and although it provides free access to all users, you need to pay to join as a citizen in order to access different areas. The biggest complaint about it seems to be that the graphics are out-moded and that building is complex – it takes more time than in Second Life, causes lag, and the ability to create external detail on the buildings is limited.

## Twinity

This 3D immersive world was developed in 2008, and provides accurate virtual versions of real-world cities. To date Berlin and Singapore are active, with London soon to follow. Users of this world tend to comment that it is difficult to move around and there is a tendency to feel stuck in one place.

## Blue Mars

This is defined by the designers as a free massively multiplayer virtual world. It comprises independently operated cities each of which has par-ticular themes and activities. The Blue Mars platform and development tools continue to be developed by Hawaii-based Avatar Reality to allow people to create virtual worlds, games, homes and simulations. The com-pany Avatar Reality is currently working with a number of developers (mostly individuals and small groups) who create components such as cities and environments for Blue Mars. Registration is free as is the de-veloper kit, although some external 3D graphics software may require purchase.

## Web.alive

This is gaining ground as a browser-based virtual world. It defines it-self as 'a virtual world software application that provides an enterprise ready, network secured virtual world platform for collaboration, assisted e-Commerce and virtual learning and training applications'. In short it is a web-based tool that is embedded within web pages. It appears to be an interesting integration tool and a demonstrator is free to download but the costs may be prohibitive for higher education, especially as it has a strong commercial focus on its site.

## Younger alternatives

Second Life teen grids have been used very successfully, one example being the Schome Park project. However, one of the difficulties with this is that there is no transition between the teen grid and the main grid. Thus it is difficult for students who have been active and familiar with the teen grid when they are suddenly asked to leave having reached the age limit. It also takes time for staff who want to teach in there to use it in further education or to communicate with potential university students, who may not be able to gain access to it. Other environments such as <u>Club Penguin</u> and <u>Habbo</u> tend to be little more than avatar chatrooms – although they can be a useful and safe space for younger children interested in social networking.

## Conclusion

This chapter has suggested strategies for developing Second Life and mechanisms for sustaining its use. While there are other alternatives to Second Life, the ability to create objects and learning space easily is something that appeals to staff and is relatively straightforward for most academics. However, the use of Second Life for effective learning does require considerations beyond funding and collegial support; it requires good planning and sound design, which is explored in the next chapter.

# 3 Planning and designing learning in Second Life

## Introduction

This chapter explores the choices and decisions that need to be made when deciding how to plan, design and implement learning in Second Life. It begins by examining the kinds of issues that need to be considered such as the needs of students, when and how it might be used, and recommends theories and ideas that might inform teaching. The later section considers design issues and presents ideas and strategies for ensuring sound design. It suggests what works and what doesn't and offers guidance for designing effective scenarios and activities.

## Choices and decisions

One of the difficulties but also one of the delights of using Second Life in higher education is that much of what has been undertaken has been instinctive, unplanned and innovative. The result is that many innovators have challenged the boundaries and possibilities for learning in higher education, but the difficulty with this position is that much of what has been implemented through spontaneity has provided little in the ways of design guidance and templates for others to follow. Often in higher education the starting point for considering how a module or programme is designed is to focus on what content should be covered. Yet in Second Life the focus shifts and there is a tendency to think instead about 'How can Second Life be used for learning?', which is quite a different stance. Some of the issues about choices and designs include:

### What do you want students to learn?

Although the answer to this question will inevitably vary across the disciplines it is a question that bears exploration when designing learning for Second Life. It is important to consider if you want students to build and script, learn about inworld sociology and practices, or to learn skills, capabilities and content through particular activities in Second Life. To concentrate on what students are to learn will help to develop a focus on both the medium and the message of learning in this environment. For example, the use of the medium itself tends to interrupt our thinking about how content might be managed and presents a challenge to do it differently. The message then to the students is that deconstructing knowledge and practices is part of the learning in this environment. Furthermore it is important not to underestimate the value of learner-led and created activities that this environment seems to prompt in students.

### Who are the learners?

It is important to consider the students in terms of age, experience and what the focus of their learning might be. For example, Rappa et al. (2009) suggest that the role of a teacher could be seen as a mediator or mentor to the students, and present a framework which suggests that the three dimensions – teacher, learner and ICT – need to be synchronised. They do suggest that this framework remains too narrow since it does not reflect the capacities of Second Life to simulate real-world circumstances. This and other literature (for example Hemmi et al., 2009) would seem to indicate that teaching in Second Life needs a different framework to guide effective teaching. Discussion about how to equip students is discussed in detail in Chapter 7.

### What are the needs of the students?

Student cohorts obviously vary according to course, culture, discipline and country, but ensuring learners have the confidence to learn through Second Life at the outset is important. Examining prior experience, technological competence, understanding of equipment, bandwidth and expectation of teaching and learning, as well as time zone differences, will be an important factor in planning and organising the learning activities. As increasingly many students will be studying part-time at a distance it is likely that many will be tired and will take time to adapt to the module and hours of study. Students with additional learning needs will require support in terms of podcasts and the use of speech (rather than text chat) in Second Life. Students who have not learned through Second Life may experience disjunction, the process of becoming stuck in learning. Acknowledging to the students the possibility of disjunction and aporia, and prompting them to discuss their views of themselves as learners will not necessarily solve or prevent a sense of being stuck and perplexed, but will enable them to see that their feelings are not uncommon on the course.

### How many students will it be possible to teach this way?

Although Second Life can be used for face-to-face, distance and blended programmes, it is essential to realise that its use will not mean it is possible to teach more students faster and better. Often Second Life teaching takes longer than face-to-face teaching, although students can be left to do many activities alone and will learn much from one another. Group sizes should be kept small (8–10) so that learning can be maximised. Whether you are undertaking building seminars, discussion groups or problem-based scenarios, students work best in small teams.

## How do you see your role as a teacher in Second Life?

It is often difficult to shift away from being a tutor who offers students plenty of information and endless references, but facilitating learning in Second Life often involves a move towards being someone who facilitates the learning rather than just provides information. It is important to consider your role before you start, because if you want students to learn differently from the way they expect in real life it will be important to adapt your approach. Below is a somewhat utopian view of how I wanted to run a Masters module in Second Life and my reflections on how I saw my role initially. Perhaps unsurprisingly it did not quite work out that way… see Figure 3.1:

---

Since the module is PBLonline at a distance I see myself as a facilitator whose values centre on education as the practice of freedom and the ideals that students (and staff) need to 'transgress those boundaries that would confine each pupil to a rote, assembly-line approach to learning' (hooks, 1994: 13). The approach I would take to facilitation would therefore be from a Freirian perspective focussing on the dialogue between the teacher-learner and the learner-teacher. Freire (1974) regarded the teacher as a facilitator who is able to stimulate the learning process, rather than one who teaches 'correct' knowledge and values. Thus e-facilitation will be adopted rather than e-moderation (Appendix 2, Savin-Baden, 2007a) since this reflects the values and philosophy of PBLonline. In terms of the students I believe my sphere of influence and responsibility would extend to:

1) awakening students to values and ideologies that are embedded in texts
2) prompting them to challenge common practices within their discipline or profession
3) supporting them in deconstructing practices that perpetuate conditions that are unacceptable, such as ageism and gender stereotyping
4) challenging them to explore who is represented and who is omitted
5) encouraging them to interrogate texts for what is included and what is excluded from the dominant discourse.

---

**Figure 3.1** Perspectives on anticipating facilitating learning in Second Life

## How much teaching time will you use for it?

One hour? Thirty hours? How much time will you facilitate? How much time do you expect students to learn alone? This needs careful planning as once the session begins, time seems to evaporate. It is best to plan for a two hour session with the assumption that students can stay inworld after the session to continue longer if they so choose. Remember too that when students are new to Second Life (newbies or noobs) activities and actions take longer, and you need to allow time for everyone to become reasonably comfortable inworld (although a few never reach that point).

## When will you use it?

Considering which area of the programme to place the Second Life learning seems to be largely related more to tutor confidence and control than any particular logical reasoning. There are at present a variety of programmes from first year modules in computer science to second year geography and many MSc programmes – so it is being used across a spectrum of courses and levels across higher education. However, what is essential is that staff and students are prepared properly at the outset – which is discussed further in Chapters 6 and 7.

## Which theories will inform your design?

When deciding to use Second Life for learning it is important to consider not only the purpose of using the medium but also the pedagogy. There is a tendency to just adopt the approach of saying to colleagues that learning in Second Life is 'just experiential', whilst nodding towards Kolb's learning cycle as a point of reference. Perhaps a better approach is the one exemplified by a colleague who recently asked, 'How can I ensure that what I plan and design in Second Life will work effectively?' The way forward is to consider the relationship between the media and the pedagogy. Table 3.1 may be useful for designing for learning in Second Life:

## Which activities will fit best with your discipline?

To begin with it is helpful to use exploratory activities and quests so the students become familiar with Second Life. Nevertheless discipline-based pedagogies do affect which activities will work best with your subject. For example, using a whiteboard to get physics students to work in teams to solve a math problem, connected with a scenario concerning the correct temperature for melting chocolate in a sweet factory, is likely to work well.

**Table 3.1**   Theories to inform design

| Pedagogical approach | Related theory | Theorist | Types of Second Life activities that match |
|---|---|---|---|
| PBL Constellation 9 Problem-based learning for transformation and social reform | Critical pedagogy and social action | Freire (1972, 1974) hooks (1994) | A scenario that prompts students to examine structures and beliefs, such as the scenario below (Example 3.2) about Second Life being a panoptican |
| Activity-led learning | Complexity model | Barnett and Coate (2005) | Team-led activities such as designing a set for a production of *Hamlet* |
| Co-operative learning | Co-operative education | Heron (1989, 1993) Johnson et al. (1991, 1998) | Defined by team in relation to assignment |
| Dialogic learning | Community action | Mezirow (1985) Flecha (2000) | Student-led learning teams that focus on discussion and reflection |
| Action Learning | Change management | Revans (1983) | Group-led discussion and reflection on action |
| Project-based learning | Cognitive learning theories | Vygotsky (1978) Ausubel et al. (1978) | Tutor-set, structured tasks, such as building tasks |
| Inquiry-led learning | Discovery learning | Bruner (1991) Dewey (1938) | Students decide on their own about issues that emerged during a practice or fieldwork component of their course, and they set their own objectives as to what they want to learn |
| Game-based learning | Experiential learning | Gee (2004) Kolb and Fry (1975) | Trivia games, role play, simulations |
| Leaderless group discussion | Humanism | Rogers (1969) | Student-led discussion |

Whereas designing, creating and experimenting with sets is more useful to theatre studies.

### What kind of activities will you use?

Traditionally in higher education the lecture and seminar are the most commonly used teaching approaches. Yet such methods do not work in the same way or as well in Second Life – even though many staff still carry them out. Adopting Second Life should challenge staff to consider what approaches will help students to learn best through this medium. Table 3.2 explores some teaching methods and suggests their relative value for Second Life.

## Designing learning in Second Life

There needs to be a rethinking of technology for learning since the current state of play is one of 'just implementing' technology with little design for learning or theoretical basis. Whilst it is exciting and interesting to use and develop new media there often appears to be little critical stance or critical edge about how, why, when and where practices are implemented. What this seems to be leading to is a culture of development and demonstrations on the conference circuit, rather than positioning innovation and its evaluation from a critical stance. It almost seems as if we need new media pedagogies that ensure the media and the message match.

## What works?

Some of the things that seem to work particularly well are:

- Tours of Second Life
- 7 minute streamed lectures
- Well designed problem-based learning scenarios in a small group (4 students)
- Building group with 6 students
- Individual quests followed by group discussion
- Student-led performances and shows, such as short plays, scenes or fashion shows.

There are also a number of websites such as <u>fablusi</u> and <u>unigame</u> that assist with designing scenarios. Fablusi is better for scenario development as unigame is more of a series of training programmes to encourage familiarisation with different types of online learning.

**Table 3.2**  Table of values and pitfalls of teaching approaches

| Activity | Value | Pitfall |
|---|---|---|
| Quest | Fine, challenging, innovative in design and easy to do in Second Life. | Students can get lost. Frustrating if too hard. |
| PowerPoint lecture | Can be interactive, inworld experience for distance students if space for discussion is provided. Possible for students to meet others on the course inworld. | Can be too long and so students become bored. In the main is difficult to fit it effectively with the media of Second Life. |
| Small group discussion | Encourages collaboration and critical thinking. Promotes debate. | Tendency to get distracted by other inworld events. Easy to be diverted from topic under discussion. |
| Problem-based learning scenario | Student-led, can use diverse media and fits well as an approach with Second Life. | Students can be unsure of their role. Staff tendency to over control session. |
| Building session | Promotes team interaction. Encourages sharing of expertise across cohort. | Difficult to see what students are doing wrong. Complex to instruct. |
| Virtual patient | Promotes team collaboration. Enables practising of skills not possible in real life. | Can be too linear and structured. Scenarios can be complex to design. |
| Discussion of article | Promotes student preparation for session. Prompts critical debate. Not too difficult for newbies. | Inworld distractions. Boredom if sessions take too long. |
| Debate | Helps students take a stance towards knowledge. Facilitates exploration of values and perspectives. | Hard work with text chat. Can create conflict in cohort. |
| Performance | Fits well with medium. Plenty of opportunity for innovation and experimentation. | High learning curve for students. Failure more likely compared with other approaches because of complexity. |

## What doesn't work?

Classic problems and failures include:

- Not having all the students in the environment at the same time
- Mixing experienced students and newbies together
- Long Powerpoint presentations
- Lecture-based session (20 minutes or more) with no discussions.

Boardman (2009) offers useful design suggestions for beginning to develop material for Second Life, in the following table:

**Table 3.3**   A typology of thinking about virtual world learning scenario design (Boardman, 2009)

|  | Cafe | Canteen | Dwelling | Office | Theatre |
|---|---|---|---|---|---|
| Detailed text scenarios provided | x | ✓ | ✓ | x (✓) | ✓ |
| Staff care what it looks like | x | ✓ | ✓ | x (✓) | ✓ |
| Affects learning outcome | ✓ | x | ✓ | x (✓) | ✓ |

Boardman argues that:

> whilst many academics have great ideas for learning activities in SL, and sometimes bring well-developed written scenarios for discussion, it is clear that in their thinking and their design the visual has not permeated as fully as is necessary to create successful activities. Although they often 'know' what they want, what they want it to look like and what they want it to achieve, these three things do not always work in harmony. Developing a scenario visually instead of via text-based scenarios/PBL can radically affect both the development time required and, perhaps more importantly, the learning outcomes. In evaluating a series of proposed scenarios, I identify combinations which exemplify different outcomes of this three-way conversation, providing substantial support for educators new to virtual world learning design as well as a handy checklist for experienced teachers.
>
> (Personal communication March 2010)

In particular Boardman argues that some of the questions that should be asked of staff can subsequently save designers and technologists considerable time. For example, does it matter that the dwelling is a texture or a hut? Are staff concerned about the appearance of objects and build-ings, especially if this appearance is unlikely to affect the learning out-come? In the <u>PREVIEW</u> project (which developed problem-based learning scenarios for use in Second Life and is discussed in further depth below), it did matter both that the audio sound (ringing) came from a telephone, and it was something students would recognise, so that they would realise they should touch the telephone in order to get instructions. Boardman suggests then that staff need to consider issues of design that relate to en-suring students engage, that the buildings, objects and activities are both relevant and believable, that they are easily navigable and help students to focus on what is to be learned. She suggests that the questions that need consideration are:

1) What do you want built?
2) What is the learning outcome?
3) How detailed does it need to be?
4) Do you have a picture?
5) Do you have a mental model and can you draw it?

Although the suggestions here are arguably not entirely new, what is important is that the learning activities presented here have been designed specifically for use in Second Life – not just adapted for use from old practices. However, the use of machinima, non-player characters (also re-ferred to as chatbots) and virtual performance for learning could be seen to have emerged as a result of the use of Second Life in higher educa-tion.

## Designing scenarios and activities

Designing scenarios and activities for this environment differs from the development of face-to-face scenarios or scenarios developed for use in a discussion forum. It is difficult to delineate what this means in reality initially, and staff often focus on knowledge and content coverage, rather than the way learning will be managed and the complexity of the problem scenarios. Further as David Burden at Daden suggests 'One point I think is missed but we think is increasingly vital is simply do they (*the students*) need to know it is Second Life. We create a lot of issues for ourselves by saying "we're going to use this funky social virtual tool called Second Life to teach you something boring, so please don't turn into a dragon and go flying off but just stick to the boring lesson", rather "here's our new health and safety simulation exercise – enjoy it".'

Thus in terms of design the following guidance should be useful:

## Ten top tips for scenario design in Second Life

1) Consider what it is you want students to learn – not what content you want them to cover
2) Decide how this learning will be assessed
3) Make a list of what you want them to learn (your learning intentions)
4) Think about the learning context – how the space in Second Life will look
5) Ensure the students know what they are supposed to do – are there instructions and do they know where these are?
6) Try to make scenarios interesting enough to be a challenge but not so controversial that students become side-tracked
7) Explore the extent to which formal knowledge is being provided in the course and examine how students will transfer the knowledge into the scenarios and how you will enable them to make links
8) Consider how the scenarios fit in with the rest of the programme
9) Locate ways of enabling students to illustrate what they have learnt; this may be thought of in terms of assessment or in other ways
10) Provide learning intentions that show how students may have moved beyond the intentions specified.

A project funded by the Joint Information Systems Committee (JISC) in the UK, termed PREVIEW (Problem-based Learning in Virtual Interactive Educational Worlds (see *machinima* 1)), developed and evaluated the use of Second Life with problem-based learning. In the PREVIEW project three different types of scenarios were developed:

*Information-driven:* scenarios focus on internal virtual world content, such as media technologies (video footage, images and audio) and objects within the virtual environment that provide the user with written or spoken information. The scenarios also demonstrate external content, such as web pages relevant to the situation. The scenario is presented through multiple interactive screens in Second Life. These screens output text, images, sound and video footage as necessary. The information on display changes depending on the students' decisions.

*Avatar-driven:* A typical learning scenario is set in appropriate surroundings (for example, at the patient's home or in the hospital ward) and the patient is represented by a non-player character (NPC: a scripted avatar). Initial information is given to the students by the NPC, after which the students discuss how to proceed, as in any problem-based learning situation.

Additional information may be presented on display screens (via text, image, video, animation or external links), notecards or sound streams or through the 'chat' function of any NPCs involved in the scenario. Avatar-driven scenarios use non-player characters in two forms: as 'chatbots', where the student interacts with the NPC to gather necessary information, or as avatars featured in machinima (3D videos filmed within a virtual environment) such as a pre-recorded discussion, play or critical incident.

*Mixed mode:* These scenarios use non-player characters and on-screen information so that students engage with both media in order to learn through the scenarios.

These three types were a useful starting point and helped to locate the scenarios in terms of problem typology and complexity (see Table 3.4).

**Table 3.4**   Scenario types for Second Life

| Scenario type | Level of complexity | Example | Problem type | Type of knowledge |
|---|---|---|---|---|
| Avatar driven Type 1 | Critical contestability | Stealing drugs to treat ill baby | Moral dilemma | Contingent, contextual and constructed |
| Avatar driven Type 2 | Knowledge (re)framing | Uninhabited island escape | Strategy | Procedural knowledge |
| Avatar driven Type 3 | Guided discovery | Road traffic accident | Explanation | Explanatory knowledge |
| Mixed mode Type 1 | Critical contestability | The unhelpful manager | Moral dilemma | Contingent, contextual and constructed |
| Mixed mode Type 2 | Knowledge (re)framing | The commissioner of a care home | Strategy | Procedural knowledge |
| Information driven | Linear Trajectory | Faults during construction of bridge | Fact finding | Descriptive knowledge |

Nevertheless what has become apparent is that the use of only three delineations is too narrow a stance and this needs to be developed further. However, below are some exemplars that illustrate broader complexity in terms of scenario design:

**Example 3.1** PBL Scenario in Second Life for health and social care management

**Scenario** You each represent a part of the management of an NHS residential/nursing care service – The Cedars Care Complex. There is community concern about the Clostridium difficile (C. diff.) infection and your own service is experiencing higher rates of deaths than the average. A front-page newspaper article published today is not helping matters.

**Explanation** The students arrive inworld at the Cedars Care Complex. In the office area there is a ringing phone, which when answered, is a message from the local councillor who says he will be along shortly to discuss the C. diff. crisis. There is information in the room such as web links and the newspaper article. When the students are ready, they can press a button on the table to call the councillor who subsequently arrives within a few seconds. The students then interact with the councillor (a chatbot) and discuss his concerns. When the interaction is finished the councillor is scripted to disappear and instructs them to create a plan for what to do next. At this point the students must work on a plan together for the Care Complex's next course of action.

**Example 3.2** Scenario for staff on university teaching programme

**Second Life as a panoptical space?**

'... the major effect of the Panopticon: to induce in the inmate a state of conscious and permanent visibility that assures the automatic functioning of power... Bentham laid down the principle that power should be visible and unverifiable. Visible: the inmate will constantly have before his eyes the tall outline of the central tower from which he is spied upon. Unverifiable: the inmate must never know whether he is being looked at at any one moment; but he must be sure that he may always be so. In order to make the presence or absence of the inspector unverifiable, so that the prisoners, in their cells, cannot even see a shadow...'

(Foucault, 1975: 201)

You are a group of tutors who use collaborative team learning in different universities and you have chosen to meet in Second Life to discuss the challenges and pleasures of this approach. The difficulty all of you share is how as facilitators you manage the team power dynamics without creating a learning space that seems panoptical. Use your own perspectives as a teacher and learner and any resources you have. **Create a strategy or position paper** that will be useful to you in managing power relationships and the notion of a panoptical space when using collaborative learning teams in Second Life, and which you may be able to share with others.

**Example 3.3**   Activity for students on an undergraduate nursing or paramedic programme (supplied by Kerry Cook, Coventry University)

## Aim of the session

The session aims to enable students to manage compound and simple fractures in both upper and lower limbs, and will support the participant with all the basic and background information which will facilitate the management process.

## Learning intentions

On successful completion of the session the students will be able to demonstrate achievement of the following learning outcomes:

1) Describe the structure and function of the skin, upper and lower limbs.
2) Differentiate between compound and simple fractures.
3) Examine a patient with compound and simple fractures.
4) Manage difficult circumstances.
5) Treat a patient with compound and simple fractures.
6) Communicate with the relevant personnel to plan for patient hospitalisation.

## Case scenario

Alex is a 30-year-old male working as a car designer/painter, married with two children. He prefers to use his motorcycle rather than his car as it is faster and more manoeuvrable in traffic, since he is usually travelling to and from work during the rush hour. One day he had an appointment with a new client and particularly wanted to be punctual, as there was the chance that the client would bring in a lot of extra business. At 8.30 am on a very busy road he was in collision with a truck, whose driver was trying to avoid a car and did not see Alex alongside him on his motorcycle. Alex was thrown from the motorcycle and landed on the road. Inevitably the accident caused disruption to the traffic and the area became severely congested.

## Actions

Your station received an emergency call reporting the accident and the place where it occurred. The operation room directed the crew to the site of the accident and you were informed that the area was congested and the traffic static. You are the leader of the crew.

1) What is your plan of action?
2) On arrival at the scene, what is your plan of action?

**NB:** from your first observation of Alex, his left arm is injured and bleeding, he is conscious but in severe pain.

However, what is also important is capitalising on the opportunities to use different media within Second Life, such as machinima which are useful for role play and the development of scenarios that can be used across a variety of settings.

### Designing machinima

This term was developed to combine the words machine and cinema. This development emerged from the work of cinematographers who began to combine animation and film. In Second Life there is machinima film footage taken inworld and whilst they can be used for filming learning, collaboration or theatre for research and teaching purposes, they are more often used as part of a learning scenario or demonstration. For example, rather than using real-life actors to play out a scene such as an incidence of violence or medical procedure, which may take a few days to film, they can been filmed in Second Life with avatars. This is more cost effective than using real actors since it takes less time and if the script does not work or things need to be changed, it is considerably easier than asking actors back. A further advantage is that using machinima means that real life people are not imported into immersive spaces and therefore there is a sense of the medium being used not interrupting the learning. In practice making machinima involves the following steps:

1) Decide on the purpose of the machinima – for example is it to be used for teaching, demonstration, simulation or as a learning activity?
2) Consider the audience and how they will be engaged
3) Design it with a clear pedagogical focus, so that it reflects the learning intentions of the module
4) Cost it
5) Write the scenario
6) Design the script
7) Build required sets
8) Make the animations
9) Set the context
10) Work out the time scales – time to shoot it, adapt it and retest it.

An example of planning and designing a machinima is presented in Table 3.5, for the following scenario:

***Lucky You!*** (with thanks to Pramod Luthra for the use of this scenario) (Machinima 2)
Dr Tracey Smith is a 27-year-old very attractive single blonde who currently works in the X-ray department. Her appearance is generally

**Table 3.5**  Planning and designing a machinima

| Title | Lucky you! |
| --- | --- |
| Purpose | To promote discussions between colleagues about sexual discrimination in the workplace |
| Audience | Junior doctors |
| Engagement | Use of fast-paced short clips that are both challenging and provocative |
| Pedagogical design | Problem-based learning format (constellation 9, Savin-Baden, 2007a) |
| Focus of scenario | Relationship between colleagues in workplace in terms of acceptable and unacceptable behaviours and practices |
| Script | Conversations between 3 pairs of people, filmed consecutively to make a story, interspersed with reflection from main character |
| Context | 4 contexts<br>- X-ray department<br>- office<br>- hospital corridor<br>- hospital tea room |
| Time scale | Assuming contexts are built or can be easily adapted<br>- 1 day for script development<br>- 1 day to film<br>- 1 day to edit<br>- 1 day to test and edit |

immaculate as she is very trendy and fashion conscious. Her male colleagues continually make sexist remarks and constantly undermine her. On one occasion, she had her bottom pinched by a male senior radiographer. She reported the incident to her consultant Dr Tyler who replied, 'Lucky you! I can't remember the last time someone pinched my bottom.'

No action was taken.

The final straw came when Dr Smith overheard two radiologists talking. One stated, 'I wouldn't mind that slapper working for me – she seems obliging.' The second laughed and replied, 'There's no way I'd want her as part of my team – there's no telling what she might get up to.' Both laughed and walked away. Tracey made a formal complaint to the Foundation Programme Director.

The key to ensuring the machinima are effective for learning is ensuring that the scenarios themselves are designed properly. It is relatively easy to shoot the machinima; the challenge is in the design.

### Shooting machinima: some practicalities

Although there are many web resources that provide information on developing <u>machinima</u> and <u>providing tutorials</u> it is worth considering the following issues before you begin:

- Make sure you have the right equipment and quiet space to film
- Plan the making of the machinima carefully so that you have the scenes and script set up and the actors are dressed and in the right place
- Ensure the actors doing the voices understand their roles and timing
- Make sure you have enough time to make the machinima so it is not rushed and requires considerable editing and remaking later
- Consider how it will be introduced to the students – does it stand alone, does it need a voiceover, will there be an introduction by a tutor or on the institutional virtual learning platform?
- Plan where it will be stationed on the university's island and whether it can be operated by anyone (open source) or if it is to be operated only as part of a teaching session.

The issue of planning and designing learning is central to effective teaching and learning in Second Life but issues of design in particular are often ignored. Staff often want to use Second Life for teaching and are very enthusiastic about the possibilities for its use, yet when asked what they want to use it for and how it might improve their teaching and student learning it becomes apparent that they have not entirely thought this through. Planning and design needs to be considered in terms of ensuring that learning will be realistic, credible, focussed on student learning and that it reflects the pedagogy of the discipline in which it is being used.

## Conclusion

Designing learning in higher education has often focused on covering content and ensuring that discipline-based pedagogies are followed. In recent years governments worldwide have taken a more performative stance focusing not just on learning objectives but learning outcomes. To promote teaching and learning in Second Life there needs to be a move away from such a stance and instead an examination of what it is that students should be learning and how best to facilitate that process in challenging and interesting ways. This chapter has explored design choices, raised questions about informing theories and offered some suggestions. Nonetheless an exploration of the way in which chosen pedagogies inform teaching and learning practices is also required, and this is considered in Chapter 4.

# 4 Teaching approaches to use in Second Life

## Introduction

This chapter presents and explores teaching practices currently used in Second Life across a variety of disciplines from theatre studies to health. It begins by exploring ways of reusing current practice such as lectures, seminars and problem-based learning in Second Life and discusses the relative values of reusing such formats. The second section of the chapter suggests new ways of considering what learning might be in Second Life, suggesting that new media and different practices might be adopted. It draws on current work being undertaken and also suggests new formulations of learning that might be better suited to use in Second Life than current practices.

## Lectures

One of the easiest options in Second Life is to undertake a lecture. This can be done in a number of different ways.

*Using a lecture capture system* such as Echo 360, to take a standard lecture from real life and streaming it into Second Life. This means that any lectures that have been captured and are in a university repository can just be played in Second Life by setting up a media player in Second Life. However, in order to do this you will need:

- to be the landowner or administrator of a property within which you can play the captured media
- to have files compressed using QuickTime format, and for QuickTime to be installed on your computer
- the film to exist as an active URL link on a hosting web server.

It is also possible to stream live into Second Life, which is useful for distance classes. There is considerably more detail about video streaming in the Second Life Wiki.

*Putting up a screen in Second Life* by using AngryBeth's Whiteboard and then uploading PowerPoint slides. Giving a PowerPoint Presentation in

Second Life is a useful starting point. However, with the advent of changes promised for Second Life in mid 2010 through Viewer 2 it will be possible to drag and drop PowerPoint into Second Life via GoogleDocs or SlideShare and also use GoogleDocs, or something similar, as a whiteboard in Second Life. This means that it is possible to give a real-time lecture in Second Life using your avatar, with your students joining you for it in Second Life. In practice the images are uploaded as textures, and the slide order is controlled by file name, so it helps to put the image files in the same order as you want to run the PowerPoint presentations. This also means that for students who are neither able to get into Second Life nor attend the lecture, the PowerPoint slides can be put on the university virtual learning environment for them to access. The lecture can also be then recorded as machinima for reuse so that students have access to both the slides and to what was said verbally.

Although using lectures in Second Life is both common and popular, it is questionable as to whether this is the best use of immersive virtual worlds. For international conferences, streaming the keynote speeches into Second Life means fewer people need to travel and a wider audience is reached. However, in terms of university teaching in general, there is a tendency for staff to present long and often complex lectures which rather destroys the flexibility and playfulness that is evoked by the environments. Whilst lectures do have a place in Second Life I would argue it is a small one, and indeed if they are used it is better to do short (10 minute) presentations that prompt debate and discussion, so offering opportunities for critical debates.

## Seminars

In terms of teaching in higher education the seminar is perhaps one of the most appropriate ways to learn in Second Life. There are different types of seminars that can be used and some work more effectively than others:

*Reading-based seminars* – these are perhaps the mostly commonly used types of seminars in Second Life (apart from building seminars). Here students are provided with a list of readings for each week of the module – often as many as six articles, however two is preferable in terms of generating quality discussion. Students are required to come to the seminars having read the articles in order to discuss them. This can be quite a demanding seminar to run in Second Life and is increasingly one that is used with audio communication rather than text because of this.

*Building seminars* – any staff using Second Life tend to find that even if students do not need to create, design and build in their course, there is still interest in not only changing appearance but also learning how to build. Even if it does not seem to be an important piece of 'content' to cover, I suggest that a basic building seminar is useful for helping the students to learn to work together as a team, and it also helps to overcome their fascination with building early on. Further, there have been examples of students using building in Second Life to learn in ways that may have been initially unexpected. For example, students studying philosophy on the Open Habitat project (Talbot, 2009) built environments to explore how philosophical debates may have been conducted in particular environments and how this would have affected issues of identity.

*Presentation seminars* – this is where students have been allocated an individual topic related to the current area of study in their course or module, and are asked to present an overview to the group (for 3–5 minutes) which is then used as the starting point for a discussion. This can be done either by having just two or three students present each week or by having the whole seminar group present consecutively. It is usually better in Second Life to only have two or three presentations as this ensures maximum opportunity for debate, and helps to prevent the situation occurring where the session feels as if it is just a series of short lectures given by students.

*Follow-up seminars* – these seminars are usually used as more of a Socratic approach to teaching, where students have the opportunity to raise questions with a tutor following a lecture. Here students not only debate and clarify terms but also have time to check their understandings and space to ask about assignments.

## Problem-based learning

There remains an assumption worldwide that there is just one method of problem-based learning (PBL) that should be used in one particular way, invariably the early model as described by Barrows and Tamblyn (1980). Yet there are numerous different types which can be adapted to reflect the discipline into which they are placed. In problem-based learning the starting point for learning is always a problem, situation or scenario – rather than teacher-driven knowledge. Facilitated by a tutor, students are expected to work in small teams to work out what they need to know, and discover how to manage the situation effectively. However, given the range of variations it is best to begin by considering constellations of PBLonline and then moving onto forms of PBL specifically designed for use in Second Life.

The idea of locating different formulations of PBLonline as a series of constellations is because many of them relate to one another and overlap in particular configurations or patterns. Problem-based learning is a learning approach that is often understood to be either a very loosely managed form of learning where students are not guided at all by tutors, or one that is a very tightly controlled form of problem-solving activity. In the last decade problem-based learning has changed considerably. Problem-based learning was a once relatively stable and clear approach to teaching, with a number of models and variations which shared similar philosophies and perspectives, but now the current landscape is diverse, complex and contested. The result of such diversity is a landscape of both confusion and enthusiasm, which has resulted in overlapping concepts, terms, ideas and views about what once counted as problem-based learning. Further, they also share characteristics in terms of some forms of focus on knowledge, more or less emphasis on the process of learning and the fact that each constellation begins by focusing on some kind of problem scenario. The notion of the constellation helps us to see that there are patterns not just within the types of PBLonline, but across the different constellations, see Table 4.1.

When problem-based learning is designed specifically for Second Life there is a focus on moving the pedagogy and the curriculum towards a sense of uncontaining learning and reducing ordering, in ways that fit better with PBL in Second Life than more traditional models. Students then move away from more traditional models of online learning that focus on content coverage and ordering the learning in particular ways. In particular it encourages staff and students to explore the way in which the digital spaces that are created for staff by commercial organisations (that can be politicised and contained by universities) and used by students enables, but perhaps more often occludes, ways of seeing where information is located. Thus programmes, modules and scenarios are designed in such a way as to prompt students to examine the underlying structures and belief systems implicit within a discipline or profession itself; in order not only to understand the disciplinary area but also its credence. Thus there is a shift away from scaffolding learning and moving towards the exploration of learning values, which will be discussed in-depth in Chapter 5.

## Using machinima with PBL scenarios

Machinima are used in a variety of ways. For example, in the PREVIEW project they were used as components of the problem-based learning scenarios, where students were given the context of the scenarios to be studied and were then played the machinima. The setting was a care home and the machinima demonstrated the different perspectives of all those involved in complex and difficult situations. Other machinima were developed for helping junior doctors to discuss issues of discrimination in the workplace, such as *Lucky You*. This was particularly effective since it enabled avatars to be adapted to reflect gender stereotypes and assumptions.

**Table 4.1** Constellations of Problem-Based Learning Online

| | Constellation 1 Problem-solving learning | Constellation 2 Problem-based learning for knowledge management | Constellation 3 Project-led problem-based learning | Constellation 4 Problem-based learning for practical capabilities | Constellation 5 Problem-based learning for critical understanding | Constellation 6 Problem-based learning for multimodal reasoning | Constellation 7 Collaborative distributed problem-based learning | Constellation 8 Co-operative distributed problem-based learning | Constellation 9 Problem-based learning for transformation and social reform |
|---|---|---|---|---|---|---|---|---|---|
| Problem type | Linear | Designed to promote cognitive competence | Project-led | Practical resolution | Knowledge with action | Managing dilemmas | Defined by team in relation to practice | Defined by team in relation to assignment | Seeing alternatives |
| Level of interaction | Problem-focussed | Problem-focussed | Project team | Practical action | Integrations of knowledge and skills across boundaries | Taking a critical stance | Collaborative | Cooperative | Exploring structures and beliefs |
| Focus of knowledge | Mode 1 | Mode 1 | Mode 2 | Mode 2 | Mode 1 and 2 | Mode 3 | Mode 4 | Mode 4 | Mode 4 and 5 |
| Form of facilitation | Directive | Directive | Project management | Guide to practice | Coordinator of knowledge and skills | Orchestrator of learning opportunities | Enabler of group reflection | Consultant to team | Decoder of cultures |
| Focus of assessment | Solving of problem | Testing of knowledge | Project management | Competence for the world of work | Use of capabilities across contexts | Integrate capabilities across disciplines | Self analysis | Collaborative self-peer-tutor | Flexible and student-led |
| Learning emphasis | Achievement of task | Knowledge management | Completion of project | Development of capabilities | Synthesis across boundaries | Critical thought | Effective team work | High team support | Interrogation of frameworks |

Although the examples above reflect the use of machinima for problem-based learning, they can also be used as part of performance, for example in theatre, as discussed below. At a practical level machinima can be used as demonstrators – either to showcase medical procedures or to demonstrate the use of Second Life itself. Often when presenting examples of how, where and when to use Second Life to conference audiences around the world, getting a connection to Second Life or ensuring the graphics and bandwidth are sufficient means that live demonstrations can be risky. Using machinima to demonstrate ways of using Second Life is often easier.

## Demonstrations

Demonstrations can take many forms in higher education, but are perhaps most associated with science subjects such as physics, chemistry and engineering. The purpose of demonstrations as Brown and Atkins (2002) suggest, is to underline and explain theoretical principles that have been presented in lectures. The advantage of providing demonstrations in Second Life is that students can undertake them themselves safely and the demonstrations can be used many times without incurring extra time and cost. The other advantage is that it is possible to demonstrate things in Second Life that it is not possible to demonstrate in real life, such as explosions in space and moon walking.

## Film and video

As with demonstrations, visual media have been used for teaching, often to begin a debate and encourage students to consider their stance. The availability has obviously increased with the advent of the Internet and this also includes the increasing use of video capture of lectures. Perhaps one of the best resources is <u>HERMES</u>, provided by the British Universities Film and Video Council, which lists programmes in most academic subject areas. Streaming film and video into Second Life is common practice, but is not without its difficulties. A helpful guide is provided on <u>Streaming video into Second Life</u>. However, as with other teaching methods it is important to question how useful this is for student learning, whether it needs to be done in Second Life and if it might be better to provide the links on a discussion forum. Nevertheless short clips can be useful as a starting point for seminar groups, and is perhaps a useful starting point for those undertaking language teaching in Second Life.

## Simulations

Simulations have been used in real-world settings for many years for learning and practising skills. Perhaps the most notable and complex simulations are those used for aviation and space programmes. Growth in the use of simulations occurred in the 1980s particularly in the areas of medicine and health care with the increasing use of skills labs. More recently other high quality simulations have been developed, such as those provided by Medical Education Technologies Inc. Simulations are very effective for trial and error learning – where skills can be gained through practice, but one of the difficulties is that for the skill to be effective it needs to have been practised across contexts. For example, Eva et al. (1998) have suggested that the problem-solving theories concerning ways in which students transfer knowledge from one context to another fall into two broad areas: abstract induction and conservative induction. Abstract induction presumes that students learn principles or concepts from exposure to multiple problems by abstracting a general rule, thus it is independent of context. Conservative induction assumes that the rule is not separated from the problem context but that expertise emerges from having the same principle available in multiple problem contexts. What is important then is that practice occurs across different types of context. Studies in both psychology and medical education have found that transfer from one context to another is less frequent and more difficult than is generally believed. Schoenfeld (1989) showed that students trained on a geometry problem did not transfer their knowledge to solving construction problems because they believed that such problems should be solved using trial and error. Eva et al. suggest that transfer of knowledge between problems of the same domain (such as chest pain) is much more likely when the context has changed. This means that we should give students the opportunity to practise solving similar problems in the Second Life classroom; in this case an example would be different clients with various types of chest pain. However, recent research on virtual reality and simulations would seem to suggest that transfer is more likely from virtual situations to real life situations than early work on transfer across different real world settings had previously implied. For example, the level of motivation to learning that immersion provides is also important. Dede (1995) argues that the capacity to shape and interact with the environment is highly motivating and sharply focuses attention. Similarly Warburton (2009) indicates that the immersive nature of the virtual world can provide a compelling educational experience, particularly in relation to simulation and role-playing activities.

It is important to recognise that there are three dimensions to the design of a simulation in Second Life:

*The context of the activity or task*: this needs to be realistic and something to which students relate

*The content:* the domain of knowledge that relates to the area of the discipline being studied

*The schema or deep structure:* the 'underlying game'. For example, it would seem that in the learning process many students fail to locate what Perkins (2006b) refers to as the episteme, or underlying game (what it is that is required by the tutor). Staff attempts to communicate the underlying game have taken a number of forms. For example, Kinchin et al. (2008) suggest that providing information in chains is unhelpful to students and are merely procedural sequences. What they argue is that teaching students within a linear lecture structure fails to help students to link different knowledges together. Instead we should teach networks of understanding, illustrating how knowledges and practices are connected so that knowledge is integrated and holistic.

The advantages of using simulations in Second Life are:

- Through them it is possible to create a sense of reality and immersion – which will be discussed in Chapter 5
- Once they have been designed they are easy to set up and play again. This means if they are designed well students can practise skills at any time. Indeed paramedic students on the PREVIEW project valued the opportunity to use the scenarios to practise for examinations
- It is possible to practise skills and undertake experiments that would be too dangerous or complex in real life
- That students can be placed in situations that are not possible, such as deep space or within an illness, such as being able to experience a psychotic episode
- Once simulations have been created they are inexpensive to adapt and reuse
- By using holodeck technology – changeable environments where the scene changes at the touch of button, it is possible to cater for different and easily changeable simulations. For example, although not technically a simulation, Coventry University island has one healthcare environment that caters for different clinical management scenarios. It consists of a virtual care complex that caters for make-believe patients with learning disabilities, within which a 'holodeck' is placed. This holodeck changes scenes according to each scenario, never changing the structure of the building but instead removing and adding interactive information or NPCs as applicable to the scenario. A perhaps more accurate simulation can be seen at Imperial College School of Medicine. Here an

interactive scenario has been developed around an intravenous infusion pump that had been badly mismanaged just prior to the user entering the simulated ward. Students undertake routine safety tasks, engage with other (automated) members of staff and interact with an (automated) patient as well as the medical device during the scenarios.

## Virtual performance

The use of virtual performance is being used for teaching theatre and performance but also for exploring virtual spaces as media. By creating Second Life theatres students can create and plan performances and design and test sets before they are used in real life. However, perhaps some of the most interesting work in this area is the use of SL performance and mixed reality performance. An example of Second Life performance is provided by Chafer and Childs (2008), who deconstructed two scenes from *Hamlet* that were performed live in a recreation of the Globe Theatre in Second Life to an inworld audience, by a troupe of performers known as the SL Shakespeare Company. Chafer and Childs found that there was a need for new skills such as dovetailing during virtual performances in order to compensate for the time lag across countries and networks. Dovetailing meant the performers found that they had to begin their line before the end of the previous one to prevent gaps which would have slowed down the performance. What they also found was that issues such as proxemics, representation and understanding rules, gestures and conventions were all issues they had not initially realised would have such an impact on virtual performance. They argue however that:

> A performance designed around the strengths of a virtual world and in which the technology was an element to be explored and integrated into the experience would be less problematic. In those circumstances, the intrusions of the technology would be a factor to be experimented with and experienced, rather than distractive interference with the performance...An example of the type of performance in which the technology is foregrounded is given here:
>
> *J: something which is more along the lines of the telematic performances where we have real people in a space and we have virtual people in a virtual space and we find some way of mixing the two together, but without worrying about a particular narrative or whatever, but essentially treating it like a drama game that we play with but is also a technical game at the same time.*
>
> (Chafer and Childs, 2008: 102)

In terms of mixed reality performance, Chafer and colleagues are now creating real life performances in conjunction with avatar performance.

## Virtual debates

The use of debates in face-to-face classrooms is still quite underused except perhaps in areas such as business studies and law. Yet debates are very effective in Second Life whether using voice or text chat. This is because instead of the tutor just discussing an issue or article, a debate structures and formalises the discussion in a way that prompts students to take a critical stance. Virtual debates can be adapted from traditional debating where the students are divided into two groups and expected to take opposing sides on an issue. Perhaps what is more interesting is for a short fast-paced debate to take place between inworld teams or between an inworld and a real world team. With inworld debates teams must be kept apart once assigned the task so cheating is prevented, and time limits are needed so interest in the debate is maintained.

## Identity reassignment activities

This activity is complex and littered with ethical issues and concerns, but it is worth considering. Second Life is an arena in which diasporas, the relocation of people away from their homeland and into foreign lands is largely ignored, and using identity reassignment activities can help students consider hidden diasporas. Although there may be many cases of identity play in both real and immersive worlds, perhaps what is more apparent is the way in which identities rather than roles are changing. A recent study by Ducheneaut et al. (2009) examined avatar personalisation in Maple Story, World of Warcraft and Second Life. The findings, he argues, indicate a focus on common avatar features such as hair and experimentation with digital bodies. Identity reassignment activities however, can be used to explore issues such as culture, gender, race, disability and age or return to newbie status. It is noticeable that almost everyone chooses to be young and beautiful in Second Life but by asking students to swap gender, become a wheelchair user or become an older person can challenge them to explore how they are treated, viewed and spoken to inworld. In practice students would be asked to change their appearance markedly and visit different areas in Second Life, such as the skiing area as a wheelchair user, in order to explore other people's responses to them.

In a recent discussion staff who have been using Second Life for a number of years were reflecting on what might occur and how they might feel if they were to dress as a newbie, because of the way they felt they would be treated, spoken to and approached. Most staff believed they would be patronised but they also noted that even if they dressed as a newbie it would be quite difficult to move as one, and this would make playing the role difficult. What this activity will do is help students to explore not only their own prejudices, but also to consider issues such as power and agency not only inworld but also in their future work lives.

## Replayable podcasts and debates

Although podcasts and replayable debates are not ideal media for use in Second Life, the opportunity of using them inworld as opposed to through a virtual learning environment such as Blackboard does have advantages. For example, students involved in activity-led, problem-based or collaborative learning can use these as learning activities and areas for discussion and debate. Currently podcasts are used in a somewhat solitary fashion (see for example Salmon and Eridisingha, 2008) and thus the material presented to students via podcasts often is not actually debated. The practicalities of uploading audio to Second Life is straightforward and audio can just be placed behind an object or if preferred a display with instructions. Replayable debates can be provided as inworld video (for example, between two experts on a given topic) or as machinima. What is important is that the media are replayable by the students so that they can return to them, reflect on or revise from them.

## Non-player character interactions

Non-player characters, more often termed chatbots, are used for a variety of reasons. Perhaps at its simplest level the chatbot is used as a virtually scripted actor for students to interact with. Here a script is created and key words are used as prompts for the chatbots. In practice this means a role is created for a chatbot in a scenario and students interact with it; an example of this is where the chatbot is the manager of a care home which can be seen on the PREVIEW YouTube channel.

Using a chatbot in this way requires purchasing one which can be bought relatively inexpensively from Daden. Alternatively, it is possible to adapt a freely available pandorabot but this would be much more wooden, and is not designed specifically in the way the Daden bots are. There has been some discussion about using chatbots in more sophisticated ways such as in World of Warcraft. For example, Jeffery (2008) developed NPCs as tutors who could also keep a record of student attainment. What is

interesting about the work of Jeffery is his argument that 'future educational MMO's [Massively Multi-user Online games] will need end user
teacher-defined quest activities' (p. 182), which suggests that in order to
use Second Life in higher education it necessarily needs to be quest-based.
Yet it is clear from the use of other forms of learning in a range of disciplines that there are many more options already in use. The main focus
of the work by Jeffery is on an avatar creation tool which includes spec-
ifying the NPC behaviour through a knowledge model (which illustrates
what knowledge and links it offers), a behaviour model (such as how it
can move and behave) and a dialogue model (for example, what its capabilities are in terms of dialogue); which does have similarities with the
specs used for the chatbots in the PREVIEW project. The difficulty with
the 'quest' mode of learning, however, is that it is based on a reward system and thus a behavioural model of learning. The advantage of the quest
model is that it focuses on both fun and achievement but the difficulty is
that behavioural models do tend to focus on the learning outcomes at the
expense of the process of learning. The consequence is that students are
less likely to experience learning transitions, such as when they learn to
challenge what counts as learning and knowledge, or when they begin to
take a critical view of their position as a learner within higher education.

## Conclusion

Teaching approaches in Second Life are many and varied. It is possible to
adapt lectures and seminars and adopt approaches such as action learning and problem-based learning. However, it would seem that many staff
are increasingly interested in developing new forms of media and innovative teaching methods to use in these flexible and experiential spaces.
Although this is both exciting and innovative, sometimes methods are
implemented with relatively little thought to the importance of the pedagogical implications, and it is to this we turn in Chapter 5.

# Part 2

# Developing your teaching in Second Life

# 5 Purposeful pedagogy

## Introduction

This chapter will suggest that interactive and dialogic approaches are largely more useful than didactic ones in this environment, and link the activities discussed in Chapter 4 to relevant related theories. It will also explore the importance of identity, emotion and immersion for learning in Second Life. This chapter will be more theoretical in its approach than earlier chapters and suggests a range of pedagogical approaches that work effectively in Second Life. It will examine the relative value of lecture-based approaches, activity-led learning and performance, as different media for learning in Second Life. The chapter begins by examining some of the pedagogical opportunities provided by using Second Life for learning and suggests the value of its use for higher education.

## Pedagogical opportunities

Most research to date has been on students' experiences of virtual learning environments, discussion forums and perspectives about what and how online learning has been implemented. Virtual world learning seems to offer opportunities to move away from scaffolding and introduce new perspectives relating to the study of the socio-political impact of learning in higher education. This is because immersive learning spaces such as Second Life are universal, not bounded by time or geography, and in particular adopt different learning values from other learning spaces (Savin-Baden, 2007a; Olsen et al., 2004; Malaby, 2006). However, there remain a number of dilemmas over the pedagogical use of Second Life as exemplified across both the e-learning community and the wider educational community. It has been widely acknowledged that virtual worlds do present educational potential in terms of role-playing, building and scripting items and fostering dialogic learning and social interaction (Savin-Baden, 2008). Despite many cogent arguments there has been relatively little pedagogical rationale put forward as support. Mayes and de Freitas have argued that 'for good pedagogical design, there is simply no escaping the need to adopt a learning theory' (2004: 6), and this is particularly so in Second Life. Others suggest the need for strong pedagogical scaffolding in order to support effective learning (Salmon, 2009) although it is not entirely clear why this is more the case in Second Life than other environments. Furthermore, there has been a notable reluctance either to situate or theorise learning in Second Life when turning to newer and emergent learning theories, such as supercomplexity (Barnett, 2000), threshold concepts (Meyer and Land, 2005; Land et al., 2008) or the conversational framework (Laurillard, 2002) – although the latter is seen as largely too structured for use in Second Life. The challenges then seem to centre not only on the technical and pedagogical issues raised by many in the field, but also the purpose and impact of using such worlds within higher education. In terms of practice, though, this text seeks to provide pedagogically driven suggestions, whilst acknowledging that both the theorising and the practices related to using Second Life in higher education are not unproblematic.

Whilst theories of learning have never been static, the distinction between and across the approaches – behavioural, cognitive, developmental and critical pedagogy, continues to be eroded. There is increasing focus in the twenty-first century on what and how students learn and on ways of creating learning environments to ensure that they learn effectively – although much of this remains contested ground. New models and theories of learning have emerged over the last decade that inform the development of learning in Second Life. For example, the work of Trigwell et al. (1999) on teachers' conceptions of learning offers useful insights into the impact such conceptions have on student learning. Yet, the work of Meyer and Land (2006), Haggis (2004) and Meyer and Eley (2006) has been critical of studies into conceptions of teaching and approaches to learning. Thus with the shift into Web 2.0 technologies, and the increasing focus on learning and interaction through social networking, it may be advisable to develop academic regulations that fit more effectively with these approaches to learning, than the current objectives model of education. For example, the focus of a learning outcomes model of education centres on a behavioural focus in terms of what the students must do and what content they must cover; what is measurable and recordable. This model is teacher-centred. Perhaps it would be increasingly appropriate to adopt a more flexible approach when designing courses for Second Life that reflect the principles and practices of social networking. An example would be the intentional model of course design, focussing on a notion of responsible learning that embraces the idea that learning, rather than teaching, is central to higher education. It is a student centred approach, so it is the 'intentions' of the teacher that are described, what the teacher 'expects'. The focus then is on multiple models of action, knowledge, reasoning and reflection, along with opportunities for the student to challenge, evaluate and interrogate them. Thus in this model effective teaching is designed to change society in substantive ways, and is discussed in more depth later in this chapter.

One of the central difficulties of adopting and adapting learning practices for use in proprietary media such as Second Life is that it was not designed to be used for higher education. Although such an obvious stance may seem somewhat trite, what I merely point up is the importance of the rethinking that needs to be undertaken about the impact this is having on learners and learning, and the resultant ways in which teaching and learning practice need to be reconsidered. With the shifts and changes in online learning, the use of online conferences and the growth of webinars, to date there have been few major shifts in the approaches and pedagogies adopted. For example, it seems that there still remains the assumption that face-to-face practices can be merged into online spaces in ways that are not problematic. The most common mistake is to run an online conference with 40 minute keynotes and 20 minute papers, thereby creating a conflict between the medium and the message.

Similarly teaching practices and face-to-face pedagogies are moved into online spaces with little consideration of the extent to which these can be related. In summer 2009 I attended a conference, and whilst the focus of the presentations was on the technology there was a sense of staff 'just implementing' technology for teaching, with little reference to designing for learning. Whilst it is both important and interesting to develop new media, there does need to be a greater critical stance towards how, when and why technology is implemented. Although there are examples of strong links between technology, for example <u>PREVIEW</u>, <u>Open Habitat</u>, <u>Sounds Good</u> and <u>Awesome</u>, there remains a strong culture at conferences of 'show and tell' rather than examining innovations and changes in practices from a critical stance. It would seem that we need new, adapted or different pedagogies for these spaces. There has to date been a focus on technology for higher education, which whilst acknowledging the importance of teaching and learning, does not engage deeply enough with solutions that are highly effective in the classroom. The trend has been for technology to lead developments in education, bringing about a debate between educationalists and technologists about how technology should be used for learning. Yet the lack of in-depth longitudinal studies in this area introduces questions about the impact of digital technologies on student learning. There remain conflicts about whether 'technology must lead the pedagogy.' Although this position would seem plausible and convincing to adopt, it denies the difficulties inherent in putting technology in the lead. Whilst the development of 'teaching technologies' such as knowledge management systems, virtual learning environments and Sloodle have produced interesting and useful developments to help teaching and knowledge to be managed in online spaces, these developments have primarily focused on surface approaches to learning (Marton and Saljo, 1976a; 1976b) and on the management of knowledge.

Human–computer interactions have been the focus of much debate (for example, Turkle, 1996, 2005; Žižek, 2005). Those such as Pirolli (2007) have argued that humans have limited ability to store information, seeming to imply that learning is about gaining knowledge or finding the right information. Yet approaches such as activity-led learning, collaborative learning and high level constellations of problem-based learning online (Savin-Baden, 2007a) remain unrealised by many staff who focus on teaching design rather than learning design. The difference between teaching design is that the former focuses on what knowledge and content staff want to teach students. Learning design focuses on what it is students need to learn (which includes a range of capabilities and knowledge) to become, for example, a good engineer or midwife. Further, the decontextualisation of teaching methods and technical developments from both the learners and the disciplines is resulting in a worrying trend towards ignoring the particularities of teaching in a given discipline (Becher and Trowler, 2001), along with the assumption that teaching and learning are necessarily the same thing. Whilst much of this can be argued for in face-to-face teaching it does seem to be particularly apparent in online settings and immersive environments. Some of the deep educational problems are:

1) The fracture between pedagogy and technology that has resulted in failure to create socio-technical solutions to learning that are immersive, adaptive, reusable and pedagogically sound
2) The misunderstanding of ways of creating effective learning situations in immersive virtual worlds such as Second Life
3) The lack of mapping of different learning activities for different disciplines
4) The failure to understand which types of scenarios work in which disciplines and which contexts, and why this is the case
5) The lack of realisation of the potential of immersive world learning to enable better learning to occur
6) The poverty of technology-enabled learning projects that are contextually-based
7) The paucity of linking educational models and theories across contexts and disciplines. For example this is evident in the lack of connection made between sense-making theories (Dervin, 1998) and problem-based learning (Savin-Baden, 2000), where the pedagogical processes and strategies are almost an exact match. For example, the argument of sense-making theory is that by using a sense-making tool, it will be possible for people to recognise a knowledge gap, seek information, analyse and synthesise

information to create an understanding, and then possibly pro-duce a task output: a report, decision or other type of output. This mirrors the problem-based learning process.

# Motivations for adopting and sustaining Second Life use

Some of the other reasons Second Life has been adopted and sustained over time, beyond the initial interest and 'gimmick phase' is because it:

- Supports distance, flexible and blended learning
- Enables learning through immersion
- Promotes dialogic learning
- Blurs power relationships in learning
- Supports creativity and fun in learning
- Prompts reconsideration of identity in learning
- Encourages exploration of emotion in learning.

## Supports distance, flexible and blended learning

Second Life allows distance learners to meet 'inworld' and collaborate around a case, with each participant having an online presence, or avatar, to aid their communication. However, Second Life also provides flexible learning by expanding choice on what, when, where and how people learn. Second Life can also be used for blended learning whereby differ-ent learning methods, techniques and resources are applied in an inter-actively meaningful learning environment. This is important at a time when interactive forms of learning are under threat from the movement towards more personalised, self-directed learning and the migration of students from campus-based to more workplace-based learning. Learning in Second Life may help, by creating online learning opportunities that are sufficiently immersive and collaborative outside the tutorial room.

## Enables learning through immersion

Although it has been recognised in both schooling and higher education that a thorough engagement in tasks results in effective learning (Bruner, 1991; Dewey, 1938; Gee, 2004) it is only recently that the notion of im-mersion has come to the fore. Games such as the Quest Atlantis Project (Barab et al., 2007), a 3D game for children, and the River City MUVE (Galas and Ketelhut, 2006) essentially seem to have embraced immersion as a central component of learning. Whilst immersion has been central to discussion and explorations of virtual reality, immersion has only become more prominent in higher education with the increasing interest in immersive virtual worlds. There is little research that has explored immersion in Second Life. However, the work of Dede (2009) sheds some light in this area. He suggests that 'immersion' can enhance education and argues:

> Studies show that immersion in a digital environment can enhance education in at least three ways: multiple perspectives, situated learning, and transfer. Further studies are needed on the capabilities immersive media offer for learning, on the instructional designs best suited to each type of immersive medium, and on the learning strengths and preferences these media develop in users.
>
> (Dede, 2009: 66)

However, it would seem that the pedagogies associated with immersion are not fully realised. There are discussions about learning being 'situated' and arguments for 'transfer' but they do not sit easily pedagogically. For example, what counts as 'situated' varies across disciplines, contexts and cultures, and issues relating to transfer are not unproblematic – as discussed in Chapter 3. The use of immersion is often difficult to simulate or 'conjure-up' in higher education, except through performance or performance art; see for example Stellarc (2009), who suggests 'with teleoperation systems, it is possible to project human presence and perform physical actions in remote and extraterrestrial locations'. Yet such immersion can have a powerful influence on learning and offers spaces where interruptions of commonly held norms can occur. The issue of engaging, absorbing and immersing students does seem to be important and certainly stories from staff and students suggest Second Life helps this to occur. Perhaps what is crucial here is that Second Life provides a form of challenging infotainment that hooks students into learning at the outset, and from there it is possible to provide them with challenging scenarios that result in immersion.

One of the increasing areas of interest raised by staff in a recent study (Savin-Baden, 2010) was that of immersion and the impact of immersion on learning. Nonetheless immersion, even on a small scale can be disarming and staff have raised the issue that anxieties can emerge when difficulties occur with their avatars, such as feeling in danger, out of control or falling in water. Certainly a strong feature of Second Life lies in the way in which the user's attention is captivated and results in a sense of immersion or presence (Robertson et al., 1997; Steuer, 1992). For example, Dede (1995) describes immersion within learning environments as the subjective impression that a user is participating in a 'world' comprehensive and realistic enough to induce the 'willing suspension of disbelief' (Coleridge, 1817). Immersion is a complex concept related to the physical senses and mental processes of the user, the required tasks within the environment and the types of interaction and technology involved (Pausch et al., 1997). Yet a highly immersive environment will lead to a sense of the user feeling 'in' or 'part of' a virtual environment as they interact with it and become absorbed or deeply involved.

## Promotes dialogic learning

Dialogic learning (Mezirow, 1985) is learning that occurs when insights and understandings emerge through dialogue in a learning environment. It is a form of learning where staff and students draw upon their own experience to explain the concepts and ideas with which they are presented, and then use that experience to make sense for themselves and also to explore further issues. The value of this approach is that it fits well with Second Life because it brings to the fore, for students and tutors, the value of prior experience to current learning and thus can engage them in explorations of and (re)constructions of learner identity. The work of Flecha (2000) is particularly helpful for use in Second Life, since he built on the work of Mezirow and presents seven principles of dialogic learning; namely egalitarian dialogue, cultural intelligence, equality of differences, creation of meaning, instrumental dimension, solidarity and transformation. Egalitarian dialogue, cultural intelligence and transformation are certainly forms of dialogic learning that can be enhanced through the use of complex Second Life scenarios.

## Blurs power relationships in learning

Learning in higher education remains a text with certain persistent patterns which are often exemplified. This can be seen by comparing discussion forums in a virtual learning environment with dialogue and discussion in Second Life. In order to explore this I undertook a small scale study of the way language was used in discussion about assessment, comparing linguistic devices used in Second Life with those in a virtual learning environment discussion forum. It seemed that power relationships tended to blur more in Second Life between staff and students. For example, tutors' expectations and the priming of students to undertake assessment in particular ways was more apparent in the virtual learning environment discussion forum than in Second Life. Much of this could be attributed to the asynchronicity of the discussion forum and the way it was organised in a question and answer format. What was perhaps more telling was the Second Life discussion where there was evidence of greater collegiality across the power relationships. Yet the requests for evidence and the directions about what was allowed and disallowed in the discussion forum seemed to impact on issues of voice and identity for students. This often resulted in silence which might be seen as students' compliance and overreliance on tutor direction. Such hidden codes indicated a certain synonymity between the medium and the message, since it demonstrated to students what actually counted as knowledge and knowing in a given field. At the same time these hidden codes illustrated the extent to which the knowledge offered is a non-negotiable given, and is in contrast to the SL experience, where the student is allowed or encouraged to take up a position towards what has been offered. Debating was something that was lost in the discussion forum but more apparent in the Second Life discussion. Perhaps the contained spaces of the discussion forum, rather than the more ungraspable spaces of immersive virtual worlds, prevent students from determining both their 'academic destiny' and their own competence. Unilateral control would seem to be at odds with worlds such as Second Life, and thus it would seem the blurring of power relationships might enable a redistribution of educational power, so that components of the curriculum become spaces of consultation for students rather than those of containment and control.

## Supports creativity and fun in learning

A strong link between pedagogy and play appears to emerge in immersive world spaces which seem to enable an exploration of the ways in which past, current and future identities are present, embodied and interact with each other in multiple ways. The move to include more fun in learning could be seen to build on earlier work, such as that of Rieber et al. (1998) who have argued for the notion of 'serious play'. Serious play is characterised as an intense learning experience, involves considerable energy and commitment and is believed to be important for the development of higher order thinking, commitment and engagement. In a recent study (Savin-Baden, 2010) issues were raised by staff about learning, play and fun as both they and students played in and learned through Second Life. Yet such staff also experienced criticism and derision from colleagues about making learning fun, despite the seriousness of learning through play. Ken taught at a post-1992 university and was teaching undergraduate students in art and design. He was less concerned with a sense of the seriousness of play and more focussed on the value immersive spaces offered in the use of fun for learning:

> The idea that Second Life is a game for me is a positive; I think there are lots of educationalists who really don't like the idea of it being called a game because that in some way they think diminishes the educational potential of it. But, the teaching I do, is

all based around games, that's all I do, that's what I teach, that's how I teach, you learn by playing. You learn by doing something and I see no harm in there being an enjoyable, playful aspect to something..., you can teach people in a way that is much more playful, that is much more open and to an extent you learn without necessarily realising you're learning something.

His argument was that education needed to be more playful, particularly in the face of an increasingly performative higher education culture. Yet he sensed criticism and derision from colleagues about making learning fun, despite the seriousness of learning through play he believed in.

## Prompts reconsideration of identity in learning

Virtual world learning seems to offer opportunities to move away from scaffolding learning in higher education since immersive learning spaces such as Second Life (SL) are universal, not bounded by time or geography, and in particular adopt different learning values from other learning spaces (Olsen et al., 2004; Malaby, 2006). Further, authors such as Turkle imply a certain troublesomeness about identity, arguing it is the 'computer culture that has contributed to thinking about identity as multiplicity' (Turkle, 1996: 178–180). Yet more recently Turkle (2005) suggests that computers are not merely objects that make our lives more efficient, but are subjects that are intimately and ultimately linked to our social and emotional lives. The result then is that computers change not only what we do, but how we think about ourselves and the world. Such suggestions would seem to be exemplified in perspectives on and studies into virtual reality and immersion (for example, Moody et al., forthcoming; Žižek, 2005; Hayles, 1999). However, what also seems to be apparent is that spaces such as Second Life bring to the fore changes about ways in which identities are constructed and deconstructed in relation to avatar positioning in such spaces. For example, a recent study by Dean et al. (2009) examined the extent to which avatar respondents related to particular characteristics of the avatar interviewers. They suggest that users of Second Life may adjust their identity to match that of their avatars. Yet there are also suggestions that 'left behind identities' in Second Life are occurring (for example, Warburton, 2008), which would also seem to be an issue emerging in the data presented below. Some recent examples of this are included in films from popular culture such as *X-Men* and *The Matrix*. Certainly Žižek (1999), in his deconstruction of *The Matrix*, suggests the possibility that the deletion of our digital identities could turn into 'non-persons' – but perhaps a more accurate idea would be one of becoming changelings, rather than deletions.

The difficulties of understanding the shifts and changes of identity in the context of teaching in Second Life and the impact that these are having on staff roles have not yet been explored in-depth, although authors such as Warburton (2008) and Carr and Oliver (2009) would seem to be moving in that direction. Identity tourism is a metaphor developed by Nakamura (2000) to portray identity appropriation in cyberspace. The advantage of such appropriation enables the possibility of playing with different identities without encountering the risk associated with racial difference in real life. Staff have certainly questioned the extent to which inworld identities have spilled over into work or home identities and impacted on or prompted reformulations of other identities in other worlds (Savin-Baden, 2010), as illustrated in Table 5.1. Yet playing at the borders of identity seemed to be an attempt to disrupt the mind/body polarity by focussing on a resituated and often repositioned body. Certainly Sinclair refers to this sense of having a left behind identity in relation to her disquiet about the relationship between her real-life and SL identity (Savin-Baden and Sinclair, 2010).

### Encourages exploration of emotion in learning

In informal discussion with staff there seems to be an assumption that more immersion means more emotional engagement which means better learning. Although this is under researched in Second Life, it is clear that emotion is one of the strongest determinants of a student's experience as it triggers unconscious responses to a system, environment or interface. Feelings strongly affect our perceptions, enjoyment and pleasure, thereby influencing how we regard our experiences at a later date. Thus in Second Life there needs to be a focus on emotional design which will involve minimising common emotions related to poor usability such as boredom, frustration, annoyance, anger and confusion, at the same time as maximising positive emotions associated with acceptance and use of the system. This will mean students develop positive relationships with the medium of Second Life and the possibility for engagement in learning is increased. Enhancing emotion in learning is also linked with issues of embodiment and presence.

## Interruption and change to current pedagogic practices

One of the challenges of introducing the use of such spaces as Second Life is that it often results in unwanted change. Many staff feel that they have too much to do already and that teaching and providing handouts should

**Table 5.1** Identities in flux

| | Characteristics | Purpose or function | Relationship with other 'identities' | Example |
|---|---|---|---|---|
| Identity tourism | Wholehearted appropriation of another identity | Playing away from other more responsible identities | Different and invariably subversive, often pernicious | Changing racial or sexual identity for deceitful purposes |
| Identity expansion | Several, but often the same voices in a wide range of spaces, a kind of expanded voice | To increase profile and voice across digital spaces | Similar, copied and stretched | The use of multiple blogs and websites |
| Identity multiplication | Different identities in diverse spaces | Identity exploration in different spaces and contexts | Different from one another but with a sense of coherence relating to real life identities | Creating avatars in different virtual worlds and games |
| Changelings | Residual identity which has a sense of being a left behind identity | A denial of current other identities or a mirroring of real-life identities due to ambivalence about them | Either dislocated from other identities or strongly copied | Avatars that are used transgressively or are used as copies of other stronger identities |
| Shapeshifters | A transformation into a different form and persona | This is unclear but usually a choice related to solving a difficulty of some kind | Usually the same, it is the form that is usually different | Shift to another form such as animagi in *Harry Potter* books, or characters in the film *X Men* |

*Source:* Reproduced from Savin-Baden, M. (2010) Changelings and shape shifters? Identity play and pedagogical positioning of staff in immersive virtual worlds, *London Review of Education*, 8(1): 25–38 (http://www.informaworld.com).

be enough. Although in general, universities do not force the use of Second Life on staff, the use of such innovations across an institution can result in questions being asked both about the innovation being introduced and also as to why change is required. Perhaps one of the most striking things about the introduction of Second Life is that it does force staff to reconsider:

- The use of current teaching practices and their relevance to a net generation
- The extent to which their current practices engage students effectively
- Whether SL can improve or add value to learning
- Whether SL is just another means of providing infotainment for students which prevents a critical stance towards knowledge.

As highlighted in Chapter 3 one of the practices that many people adopt, whether in virtual learning environments or immersive virtual worlds, is to transport real-world practices into online spaces. Whilst some of these practices will transfer to a degree, others will not. For example, in a dialogic space such as Second Life it is somewhat pointless to present students with a 40-minute PowerPoint lecture. It would be more effective to provide an edited captured lecture, or a short podcast with time for in-world discussion. Nevertheless, the main challenge of using Second Life in higher education would seem to be to help staff and students to reimagine learning in immersive settings. This will require students to break away from prior images, possibilities and ways of thinking about learning and teaching that may interfere with this radical (to them) approach to learning. To take on such a project is to create cognitive development and value orientated shifts in students' thinking, and certainly introduces a sense of the liminal into learning. To begin such a change process will require an exploration of differences in values, which is reflective of Pratt's social reforms model of education. Pratt and Collins suggest:

> Class discussion is focused less on how knowledge has been created, and more by whom and for what purposes. Texts are interrogated for what is said and what is not said; what is included and what is excluded; who is represented and who is omitted from the dominant discourse. Students are encouraged to take critical stances to give them power to take social action to improve their own lives and the lives of others.
>
> (Pratt and Collins, 2006)

This approach focuses on teaching as a collective process which challenges the status quo so that learning is seen as a process of encouraging students to consider how they are positioned through the discourses and practices with which they are expected to engage. Social reform is not only about learning with technology but deconstructing how given notions of technology and pedagogy position students. The design feature in relation to the adoption of this approach in Second Life would be to change the way people consider and value learning, away from something they believe to be normal and quite acceptable to all. Such an approach challenges the ideals of the information foraging approach (Pirolli, 2007) where knowledge is seen as having a cost structure, so that it is seen as being vital in Pirolli's model to bring the right knowledge to the right situation. However, perhaps Sharples (2009) offers a workable solution which sits between the possibly utopian view of Pratt and Collins and the linear contained model suggested by Pirolli. Sharples argues not for styles of learning or information management but for the mediation of learning. What he seems to be suggesting is that the question becomes not how does learning occur or how do students learn best, but how is learning in new spaces mediated? He suggests then that learning is not just social but socio-technical and that it is important to explore how people learn as individuals, groups and societies, so that effective systems for learning can be shared.

## Conclusion

Developing pedagogies and learning spaces for Second Life requires a new kind of professional place making where we learn to create spaces for the mediation of learning, and for repositioning learning as a shared power between staff and students. Inevitably this is likely to cause disjunction on both sides, but as Cormier suggests:

> The experience of working within a MUVE environment brings out some of the key concepts already existing inside the field or topics being covered; it exposes things that might have remained hidden in a more traditional context. This is best represented by Ian Truelove's screenshot of the virtual houses built by students, with the caption 'They're first years. They only left home 3 weeks ago. Of course they want to build themselves homes'.
>
> (Cormier, 2009)

Yet to create spaces in which learning can be mediated requires staff and students to be equipped for learning and teaching in Second Life, and it is to this that we turn in the next two chapters.

# 6   Being a teacher in Second Life

## Introduction

This chapter will offer guidance on how to equip and support staff in Second Life. It will provide introductory activities and suggest ways of getting staff accustomed to teaching in this environment. It will help staff to consider pedagogy and design questions, and suggest strategies for facilitating effective learning and sustaining the use of Second Life within the curriculum. The later section of the chapter draws on the experience of experts in the field and suggests some curriculum models of how the use of Second Life might be seen as having been implemented in line with higher education curricula.

## Getting started as a teacher in Second Life

One of the central principles of facilitating learning in Second Life is that until we understand our own pedagogical stance (what we believe and stand for in teaching and learning) it is difficult to operate effectively as a Second Life facilitator. Thus until we understand our own views about teaching, our ideas about collaboration in online spaces, and are able to consider the issues of student responsibility, it is difficult to locate ourselves in these complex spaces. A useful starting point is to ask yourself about how you see your position as a facilitator in Second Life. For example, are you

- A lecturer who wants to start by including a small amount (2 hours) of Second Life learning/teaching in your module?
- A learning technologist who is supporting staff and students in the use of Second Life?
- A lecturer who wants to move most of their teaching into digital spaces, especially Second Life?
- A teacher and user of digital spaces wanting to move into Second Life?
- A manager wanting colleagues to adopt Second Life?

Try to take time each week to become familiar with Second Life, as this will increase your confidence in the programme and will be particularly important when trying to facilitate inworld.

Second Life can be deceptive . . . It can seduce one into believing that "teaching" practices that work on the outside can be readily transposed inside. It is a sobering experience when the particular constraints of SL kick back and even the best-laid plans begin to unravel.

(Warburton, 2008)

However, there are shortcuts you can use so that you 'look right' in Second Life. You can use a personal shopper to help you find new clothes and styles – some people disapprove of this but often it is important to appear authentic even if your body language gives you away as a newbie.

Some other things to consider at the outset include:

- *Ensure you know the scenario* you are facilitating and also the learning objectives/intentions you would expect students to address in the session.
- *Try out the activities* before you facilitate inworld. It is a good idea to try them several times and if possible with colleagues, so you understand how they work.
- *Know the target audience* (in this case the students) who are going to take part in the session, so that you understand the level of knowledge they will or should apply to the scenario.
- *Represent etiquette.* Although much has been written on online etiquette (netiquette) there are differences in Second Life, particularly in relation to respecting silence, promoting student autonomy, and not interrupting when flaming occurs. This is largely because if facilitators interrupt or take control, the locus of control shifts to the member of staff and the team does not deal with the problem or conflict themselves. There is a delicate balance here, but it is important for staff to model this and also to help students develop ground rules for their own team.
- *Listen and lurk positively*. There is often a tendency, after using straightforward online learning, to retain control rather than granting it to the students. The notion of 'lurking' often seems to imply that silence and watching are inherently bad, but students often need to watch and listen in Second Life, so it is important not to confuse lurking with thinking space.
- *Recognise that being a Second Life teacher means also being a learner.* This might mean learning to develop the capabilities of a facilitator and learning new knowledge with and through the students. The process of becoming a facilitator also demands developing and understanding the way in which facilitator and team influence each other in the learning process.

- *Provide supportive interventions.* It is often easy to assume that not intervening means maintaining silence, but it is useful if students 'know' whether you are part of the discussion. Rather than just lurking, it is helpful to students if the facilitator adds some remark that illustrates they are listening and supporting the learning. Building with students and exploring different Second Life spaces with them is useful for this process.
- *Consider issues of honesty and intellectual property.* Second Life is home to numerous fringe groups and activities, and students are free agents in a free environment. The expectation would be that they should adhere to certain standards during teaching and learning sessions. However, at a more serious level it is important that there is a university agreement in place about ownership of university objects and spaces, so that issues of intellectual property do not arise.

There are also some practical dos and don'ts as presented in Table 6.1 below:

**Table 6.1** Dos and don'ts of teaching in Second Life

---

*Tips from Joff Chafer, Coventry University*

Know your teaching environment. Put in the hours in Second Life to fully accustom yourself. You wouldn't attempt to give a lecture using PowerPoint and not know how to play a slideshow, so don't attempt to teach in Second Life without knowing how to walk, fly, teleport, use your camera, talk, sit, chat and instant message and be able to talk others through the same.

If necessary have support, someone who can assist in orientating the students, for example, banning griefers (people who cause trouble and hit others).

Make sure that you or somebody you know has management rights on the land where you are working, otherwise you may find that you cannot create or make an object appear (rez) or run scripts.

Be prepared for an inworld session to take approximately twice as long as the same class would run with all participants physically present. As you and your students become more adept and comfortable with working inworld, this may speed up.

Accept that things will go wrong, this is a new platform and still being developed and added to, and that each individual will have a different set up regarding type and speed of machine, Internet connection etc.

If using slides inworld have a board that can preload the texture. This will speed up the time as each slide is loaded into Second Life and the individual users' computers prior to it being shown on the screen.

Use highlighters and markers on the boards to identify particular areas that you want students to focus on. Remember not everyone will be viewing from the same angle so when referring to something on a slide it is important to highlight it.

---

*(continued)*

**Table 6.1** Dos and don'ts of teaching in Second Life (*Continued*)

If you want everyone to see exactly the same thing from the same angle you may need to use seats that set a camera position. It is also possible to have seats that follow your camera position which can help if you want to show people around without having them leave their seats.

If possible teach using voice but ask your students to text chat. If they have their microphones open you are very likely to get echoes unless they all have good headphones.

If you have any students without sound you will need to make sure that everything is said in chat as well as voice. You can use a chat display (HUD) for this but you will need to have written the text beforehand for the class.

If you can, rehearse with a few friends before your session to get a feel of how long it will last and any potential problems.

## Be aware of the barriers at the outset

Warburton (2009) undertook a survey of literature newsgroups and blogs, and suggests that there are eight broad barriers or difficulties encountered. However, as I point out below, these are not perhaps as insurmountable as Warburton seems to imply:

1) Technical: such as managing firewall, bandwidth and hardware, dealing with lag along with the ability to become competent technically inworld.
2) Identity: this includes role management, social relationships and reputation.
3) Culture: the fact that Second Life has its own set of codes, norms and etiquette.
4) Collaboration: Warburton suggests this takes time to develop, but perhaps his most pertinent point regarding this is that the relative lack of social networking tools means that external services such as virtual learning environments (VLEs) are often needed to support the interactions between avatars.
5) Time: Often this issue about time is rather more about choice, but Warburton argues that 'Even simple things can take a long time.' Whilst this is true, to some extent new teaching approaches often demand extra preparation, so this is perhaps a more debatable concern than some of the others.
6) Economic: although as Warburton suggests buying land and other tools and textures will cost the institution, Second Life still remains relatively inexpensive compared with other technology, including VLEs.

7) Standards: this does remain a problem because of the current lack of open standards and interoperability. Yet locating them on web browsers so that they can be used on different platforms is an option many people are now adopting.

8) Scaffolding persistence and social discovery: Warburton's argument here is that 'The inworld profiles associated with each avatar provide a limited mechanism for the social discovery of others'. In short, Second Life lacks real capability for social networking. This does remain a problem, which some have sought to solve by providing links from Facebook to Second Life, but this does not really solve the difficulties. However, it is possible to create and promote group searching for people, places and events.

## Planning and design

The planning stage is almost always an iterative cycle of development, testing, changing, adaptation and redevelopment. It is helpful to consider how to orientate students, develop different kinds of materials and have an idea of how learning and teaching will take place.

### Organise orientation sessions

If possible it is helpful to develop your own orientation area that suits the needs of your courses and your institution, and to which students and staff can teleport directly. The orientation area should be spacious so that students are not crowded into a small space and unable to see anything. Orientation areas should also contain useful information that students can retain such as note cards that will remind them of functions. Make sure the orientation area includes activities such as learning to use the camera, voice control and microphones, as well as activities about getting around Second Life and finding their way back to the University Island.

One of the things to be careful of is trying to use too many different pieces of equipment early on. For example, in the PREVIEW project, soon after being presented with the problem-based scenario, whiteboards were supplied for students to write up their brainstorming and decisions. However, they tended to ignore the whiteboards, because they were more concerned with learning to learn together through Second Life and to develop an effective team, so the whiteboards became a distraction rather than a help. It is important to remember that what we as tutors feel may be helpful or what we expect students to be doing may not actually be appropriate for the place and space in which the students are learning. Again, it is easy to scaffold it for them rather than wait for them to lead the learning when often the latter is a better option. Other issues connected with planning include:

## Plan plenty of time for the students to start with

There is a tendency to organise the students to meet in Second Life, get them through orientation and then expect to be able to run a teaching session immediately. It is important that students are encouraged to take time to get used to Second Life and feel comfortable moving, flying and using text chat. If you expect them to not only start learning, but at the same time also introduce them to other facets such as head-up displays (HUDs) or sandboxes, it is likely they will forget much of what they have already learned by just being present in Second Life.

## Consider how much guidance you expect to give to the students

There is a tendency, particularly at the start of a session where students are presented with a new problem or activity, to interrupt or even pre-intervene by asking leading questions before they have had a chance to discuss the problem. It is better to wait, or to ask a gentle question such as 'What are the team thinking about this?' Joff Chafer argues:

> I think it is important to recognise when working with a group new to Second Life that different people will engage with different aspects of the environment, similarly different people will be turned off by different aspects. When I am taking a new group of students through orientation I like to let them take as long as they like over the various aspects. Invariably some will spend the entire session adjusting their appearance whilst others will have left orientation island within ten minutes and be up on stage in a pole dancing club. There is something very levelling when people first use their avatars, we become very childlike, the world is in turns frightening and exciting, we stumble around because we have not quite mastered walking, we can quickly become obsessed with the simplest of things, we have an innocence and naivety that we have long since surpassed in our real lives. I want my students to be comfortable in learning through playing.

## To scaffold or to play?

It seems that staff in higher education still have a strong need to scaffold learning and certainly development work by some would suggest this is helpful. For example, Truelove and Hibbert (2008) argue for clear scaffolding when preparing students for learning in Second Life, because their early experience indicated that students were uncomfortable in new immersive spaces. They assert:

> Students found the initial tutorial phase overwhelming, reporting feelings of confusion and anxiety, whilst failing to see the purpose of this virtual world. Observation and analysis of users identified that the requirement to simultaneously address many fundamental issues in the first few minutes of engagement was the cause of many of the negative aspects of inductions. Issues that a standard Second Life induction requires new users to address include: Creating a new identity through the choosing of a name and the dressing of an avatar, role-play with this new character (including interaction with strangers), the rapid acquisition of technical skills, economic considerations (the prospect of making money, and the fear of accidentally losing it), and the complexities of social interaction and etiquette.
>
> (Truelove and Hibbert, 2008: 363)

Yet there are questions to be asked about when, why and how scaffolding should occur. It might be that scaffolding is really being used to:

- Save time
- Relieve staff discomfort (as well as students')
- Control behaviour
- Contain learning

Although scaffolding can be helpful, it can also hinder the playfulness of learning. I would argue that it is probably more effective to encourage students to play and explore in Second Life, change their appearance and acquire things from freebie places than to scaffold the learning time. This is because some students like to change their appearance, understand moving and flying, and work out how to build. Doing this in a free and playful way reflects both the medium and Second Life. It also begins to help a power shift to occur away from staff being in charge, toward more creations of dialogic spaces for learning that have a greater sense of co-operation and collaboration than scaffolded spaces.

### Take into account how you expect groups to work

Currently collaborative learning teams are probably the most common form of learning seen in Second Life tutorials – apart from building and scripting workshops. Although it could be viewed as largely based on models of collaborative inquiry, there is still an element of facilitator control here. For example, the focus is on the development of specific levels of skills and thus small-team social skills are essential for successful collaboration in the Second Life environment. In addition to being able to communicate clearly with, accept and support all other team members individually, and resolve conflicts, students must be able to elicit each other's viewpoints and perspectives, question each other's assumptions and evidence, make decisions, manage the 'business' of the team and often make presentations to the larger year group. Activities that help to build teams online include:

- warm-up activities, such as introducing oneself, sharing something unusual about oneself or the situation
- playing team games
- doing competitive inter-team quizzes online
- sharing interesting Second Life spaces
- giving each team member a different online activity or game which they need to critique and then share with the rest of the team
- encouraging the use of Twitter, Facebook and other social networking tools.

### Reflect on what you believe are the students' roles

Learning in Second Life, although still a largely under-researched area, does require a strong focus on understanding and developing inworld interaction. If you believe you are there to tell students what they need to know, the learning experience for students is likely to be less positive than if they are seen as co-creators – so the learning is interactive. There are several models of interactional learning. And what is useful is moving students away from hierarchically structured decision-making led by tutors, to the use of teamwork and consensus for problem-solving. This model assumes that 'two heads or more are better than one' and thus students will arrive at a better solution than any single individual can supply. Interactional team learning is based on the Social Constructivist model of learning, which centres on the idea that learners construct knowledge through discourse with other members of the community, including the tutor. Thus learning is seen as being produced by the team, and not reproduced from disciplinary authority – the tutor. Much of what occurs in virtual worlds, however, tends to resemble the following types of teams:

1) The tutor-guided learning team – whereby the tutor guides the students through the learning and any problem scenario set.
2) The collaborative learning team – here students are expected to communicate clearly with one another, accept and support all other team members individually as well as resolve conflicts.

3) The reflexive team – this kind of learning team is largely based in co-operative models of learning and Freireian forms of pedagogy (Freire, 1972; 1974) thus in this type of team working together is often talked about in terms of a journey.

4) The co-operative team – involves small group work to maximise student learning. This approach tends to maintain traditional lines of knowledge and authority and is appropriate whenever the goals of learning are highly important, mastery and retention are important, or the task is complex or conceptual.

5) The action learning team – is a form of learning based on the interrelationship of learning and action, and thus the learning occurs through a continuous process of reflecting and acting by the individual on their problem with the help of the learning set.

### Consider how you see the relationship between Second Life and the rest of the curriculum

There are many different ways of designing curricula around Second Life; however the following are a few options that have already proved very successful:

### The taster option

This is a 1–2 hour session to illustrate to staff, students or other stake-holders how learning in Second Life might be undertaken. For example, it might be undertaken on a Master's module in teaching and learning, a postgraduate certificate in education or as a demonstration to senior management.

### The eventedness option

This is where learning in Second Life is seen and used as the gathering together of learning across a number of Second Life events. The notion of eventedness (a term coined by Dave White, see for example Cormier, 2009) is the idea that the shared learning of students in a Second Life space creates a particular kind of transactional learning that transcends the learning of content. The important factor is that participants need to feel they are part of a shared endeavour for eventedness to occur.

### The snack option

The snack option is probably the most common version used. This is where Second Life is used for about 2 hours per week in a specific module or unit. For example, at Coventry University a number of modules use Second Life in this way, both face to face in a computer lab and at a distance in paramedic and nursing modules.

### The immersive option

This is where Second Life is adopted consistently across a whole curriculum or programme – it can be in different unrelated modules, but more often the designs have been created together across the curriculum team in relation to each other, so that there is consistency and cohesion across the course. The focus here is that the medium of learning is also the message, so that what is seen as important is learner interaction, dialogic learning and learning how to learn through Second Life.

### Ensure you are designing effective materials

The focal point of design should be around what it means to learn in Second Life and therefore consideration of the relationship between learning and design is imperative. Materials can include an institutional Second Life Guide, activities supplied on note cards inworld, problem-based scenarios and others suggested in earlier chapters. However, scenario writing can be time-consuming, a lot depends on the case-writers, and it is not always easy to verbalise the scenarios and how they should run. One mechanism used as part of the PREVIEW project in order to work out how to design and create it was to film staff role-playing the scenarios. From this it was possible to create a script for the chatbot and work out how to design the environment in which the scenarios were to take place. A further approach is to use an external consultant as an advisor, both in terms of design and technical guidance. Perhaps what is most important is to leave sufficient time for developing and testing.

### Consider how to get students started inworld

There are a number of ways to do this and some staff choose to batch name a group of students' avatars and register them together, e.g. Coventry Watkin, Coventry Chafer, and so on. However, it is often better to ask students to register and go inworld a week or so before teaching starts, so that they are familiar with it and have undertaken the orientation. For some students providing a tutor-guided tour of Second Life is helpful. This is particularly useful for students who are fearful of travelling inworld – and it is a strategy a number of tutors have found beneficial in terms of helping to reduce student anxiety about inworld safety.

# Sustaining learning in Second Life

The difficulty with sustaining learning is the ability to provide sufficient support for staff. Whilst some support can be supplied by experts, the student flying squad and external consultants, what is also important is designing learning that is sustainable over time and ensuring that materials such as machinima are reusable, stored in an open repository and able to be shared. It is also useful to adopt forms of learning that support sustainability, such as collaborative learning groups where students work in teams, are accountable to one another and can offer peer support. However, it is also important to plan for failure and 'stuckness'.

## 'Stuckness': recognising and managing it

Many staff and students have described stuckness in learning, and more recently in teaching and learning in Second Life, as a little bit like hitting a brick wall. The stuckness is because what is being experienced seems alien and counterintuitive, and occurs because during the exploration of an idea, experience, form of learning or teaching, something troublesome occurs; and why that is, is not entirely clear. However, it seems that staff experience different types of disjunction within Second Life. Stuckness or disjunction is a 'troublesome learning space' that emerges during forms of active learning (such as dialogic learning in Second Life). Staff teaching in Second Life experience stuckness in a number of different ways, so that the conflict, ambiguity and incoherence experienced by individuals cannot be defined by distinctive characteristics, although there are some general trends.

*A moment of aporia;*[1] this is where a moment of misconception is drawn attention to by someone else, leaving the person concerned stuck, exposed and in doubt. For example, this is seen most often by staff new to Second Life, since they do not understand the codes and cultures of the environment.

*A moment of conceptual puzzlement;* this is when the self-realisation that one is stuck and does not understand how to move on results in a sense of feeling paralysed or fragmented. For example, realising that learning and scenario development for Second Life is different but not being able to articulate this or solve it.

*A cycle of stuckness;* this occurs when someone understands that they need to move away from a particular position or stuck space, but do not know how or where to move, resulting in a constant cycle of stuckness

---

[1] Aporia (Greek: ἀπορία: *impasse; lack of resources; puzzlement; embarrassment*) is a puzzle or an impasse, but it can also denote the state of being perplexed, or at a loss, at such a puzzle or impasse.

which leads to a return to the same stuck space repeatedly. For example, a tutor realises that lectures and other more traditional practices do not work in Second Life but is unable to find new approaches that do work well, and therefore uses the original approaches again and again, just trying to tweak them to make them work instead of rethinking the pedagogy completely. Although getting stuck varies across people and contexts there are ways in which staff can be supported:

- Recognise barriers to implementation
- Acknowledge to staff that getting stuck is common
- Help staff to see it as part of the development process of their learning and the development of the curriculum
- Provide structures and tools to support staff – such as design templates and questions
- Link with other staff who can provide guidance
- Develop a peer mentoring scheme
- Encourage sharing of resources and practices.

What is important about becoming stuck is to remember that although it is troublesome, it is a learning space for staff and therefore is important for the development of the pedagogy and practices in Second Life (this is discussed further in Chapter 10). Furthermore it helps them to see and understand how they use and value knowledge in their discipline, for example Perkins (2006a) has argued for three conceptions of knowing: (i) retention and application; (ii) understanding: the ability to perform what you know and thus to be able to think with what you know about; and (iii) active and adventurous knowing: a proactive conception of knowledge that requires creativity and the ability to see things differently. It is this latter conception that would seem to be important for staff in developing learning in Second Life, as it requires a leap away from bounded understanding. Issues relating to students' experiences of stuckness are dealt with in Chapter 7.

## Conclusion

This chapter has examined both the kinds of ways in which staff can be supported in designing and implementing Second Life learning, and the kinds of questions and issues it is important to consider when designing modules and curricula. However, design and implementation is only part of the challenge. The other part lies in ensuring that the resultant learning that takes place through Second Life equips students for lifelong learning, so that they are able to take up a critical stance towards their world.

# 7 Equipping students for learning in Second Life

I'm surprised you can build anything and do anything in it, really. I think that's what surprised me. But also I think it's a bit weird, like everyone is actually a person as well. Like I avoid talking to people because I always forget they're actually really people. I just think it's a bit weird.

Its inspired new ideas of where I can apply my work and it's a lot easier to try these things out on SL than in real life... knowing that people are out there and may come across it [her work in Second Life] makes me think about how my work is applied and what other people think about it...

(Truelove, 2009)

## Introduction

This chapter provides examples and suggestions about how to help students become used to Second Life and suggests some activities to use and areas for discussion with students. It begins by considering areas with which students will need to become familiar, and then suggests other areas for consideration once they have been using Second Life for a few weeks. It provides students' reflections about their early experiences. The latter section of the chapter argues that to really engage students in this environment it is vital to get them involved in the design of learning, and it offers suggestions of ways to approach this.

## Things to consider at the outset

Although some of what I suggest here seems somewhat obvious, they are things that are often overlooked by staff when they start using Second Life for teaching:

### Explain to your students why you are using Second Life for learning

Some students will find Second Life troublesome and difficult and others will dislike it for other reasons, such as the graphics. Therefore it is important that they understand at the beginning what your purpose is in using this medium – even if they disagree with you.

### Provide simple instructions – no more than one page long

Students often don't read instructions, but if you provide something short and snappy to start with this usually helps. It should include where to meet, a list of avatar names and real names and who to email or SMS if they get stuck trying to get into the first session. Students new to Second Life often forget passwords, how to access different areas and spaces and mis-understand their role, that of the team, and the instructions given to them.

### Consider how familiar they are with technology?

Are the students likely to have a wide range of technical capabilities, which may be a concern, particularly in relation to Second Life? It is helpful to know if the students undertaking the course can use email, and have the right Internet connection, hardware and graphics. Discussion around technical challenges will be an important site on the discussion board, and Table 7.1 below offers some challenges and possible solutions.

**Table 7.1**   Learner challenges

| Challenge | Possible solution |
| --- | --- |
| Assumption that learning is content focussed | Use e-facilitation model (Savin-Baden, 2007a) to move students to the position of valuing their own voices and knowledges |
| Reliance on tutor for covering content | Discuss role of tutor and use a warm-up scenario about tutor role at outset of module |
| Technology concerns | Ensure students understand technical requirements, especially with regard to Second Life. Provide forum on discussion board to share concerns, provide telephone support where necessary |
| Belief they lack academic capability | Use activities that inspire confidence and develop belief in own stance and voice<br>See not passing assessments as development rather than as failure |
| Belief they lack theoretical skills and knowledge to complete course | Use activities at the outset that help students to see the capabilities they bring to the course and ensure they work in a team to which they all bring different skills and knowledges |

*(continued)*

**Table 7.1** Learner challenges (*Continued*)

| Challenge | Possible solution |
| --- | --- |
| Self doubt and anxiety about academia | Acknowledge the existence of disjunction and aporia and provide opportunities for discussion that relates to seeing them as valuable to learning and development |
| Wanting to read everything and cover all material | Provide minimal reading at the outset, such as one short paper per week – or even none at all |
| Experiencing disjunction | Use seminar in Second Life to discuss the theory and experience of disjunction and its value in learning |
| Over/under posting on the discussion board | Assess posting for quality rather than quantity and encourage initial discussion about type and quality of postings over quantity |
| Dictating and imposing own values on the other students | Ensure teams are facilitated by tutor but are encouraged to find their own ways to manage conflict and give meaning to personal and team learning |
| Strong focus on assessment at expense of learning | Ensure assessment is designed so course engagement is required in order to fulfil requirements of assessment |

## Get students set up properly

For example:

- Give them a simple list of instructions
- Meet in a computer lab face to face if using Second Life on campus, so that you can run a very practical session and they can share ideas and experiences with one another
- Arrange to meet inworld but also be available on email or SMS, so that you can provide support if they are having trouble getting to the meeting space
- Encourage them to use Weblip (an instant messaging system that aims to connect users to other Weblip users currently viewing the same website as you) as well as Second Life, so that they can be connected to other Weblip users viewing the same website simultaneously
- Use other media that will facilitate reflection on Second Life, such as Group, which is software that allows students and staff to 'write' on sheets similar to Post-it notes and manage the movement of these electronic notes jointly within and between public and private spaces. Using this will help to develop team work and collaborative learning

- Encourage them to use Skype or other simultaneous communication during the setting up phase so they can support one another
- Make them aware of text chat contractions of words, as illustrated in Table 7.2.

**Table 7.2** Terms used in text chat in Second Life

| | |
|---|---|
| afk | Away from keyboard |
| Alt or my alt | Alternative avatar |
| brb | Be right back |
| cam | to look at as in cam around, cam over here etc., cam on down |
| cu | See you |
| fl | First life |
| im | Instant message |
| imho | In my humble opinion |
| irl | In real life |
| k | ok |
| kk | also ok |
| lol | Laugh out loud |
| np | No problem |
| psa | Pleasant Sunday afternoon |
| rl | Real Life |
| rofl | Rolling on the floor laughing |
| sl | Second Life |
| tp | Teleport |
| ty | Thank you |
| wb | Welcome back |
| yw | You're welcome |

## Spend the first session playing

This first session should be relatively unstructured and provide students with an opportunity to experiment with hair, clothes, movement and communication. This should mean that they do not spend the whole of the next teaching session dancing or changing their appearance (if that is not what they are supposed to be doing).

## Help them to understand the rules of Second Life

There are six rules that people are expected to follow, to protect the rights of other Second Life users, which are not committing:

1) intolerance,
2) assault,

3) disclosure (sharing another resident's RL personal information without consent),
4) indecency,
5) harassment,
6) disturbing the peace.

### Decide if you want ground rules

The choice about ground rules seems to vary across programmes, for example some professional courses dislike students attending class as animals. However, it is important that students help to create any ground rules so that there is ownership of them, and discussion occurs about how they are negotiated and enforced.

### Provide material on another platform as well

Using the institutional virtual learning platform is vital for ensuring students have access to materials – which can include machinima and podcasts, so that they are not excluded if they cannot gain access to Second life.

### Acknowledge rather than ignore what seem to be minor problems

Students easily get stuck and cross early on in Second Life, so providing support through the discussion forum is essential. As an MSc student I had a very early experience of being set the task of doing a treasure hunt in Second Life, and posting my frustration to my tutor (who responded with grace and humour . . . )

> I made a bit of a mess of the treasure hunt today as I thought you had hidden it obscurely inside an object on say the bar. Clearly you hadn't and I hadn't read the instructions properly. So . . . having searched Campus I went off to the library and various other odd places, only to realise that there was a poster on Campus. I have to say I got very cross and I also got stuck in some box and couldn't get out of it without teleporting myself . . .

### Provide students with a guide

There are many resources available and increasing numbers of texts and guides, but often what is needed is something very straightforward, pictorial and easy to use such as the JISC Second Life Guide. Step-by-step guides are a vital support, particularly if they include graphics, diagrams and web shots to illustrate how things appear and operate.

# Things to do in the first few weeks

### Discuss being a newbie

When students first arrive in Second Life most do not realise that they are very obvious as a newbie or that they are likely to be ignored, or targeted by griefers. Using the quotation below is often a good point for discussing these issues and helping students work out how to tackle being a newbie:

> I could tell he was a newbie just by looking at him. First, his duds – his very person – were all wrong. Nothing about him said "Wild West". All the other folks in the area were tall, proud characters in period costumes of settlers, townsfolk, gunfighters, or Native Americans. He was shorter than normal, and wearing the standard-issue white t-shirt and jeans from orientation. He did not fit in. Second, his hair was unmistakable. He had the same blonde, non-descript hairdo that I had given up months before. Third, he was having a tough time conversing. As others stood in place, turning to each other to chat, he was running up to folks and expressing his general confusion rather than trying to go with the flow of the conversation. The newbie wanted guidance.
>
> (Boostrom, 2008)

It is important to help students to understand that being a newbie has a stigmatised identity (Goffman, 1963) and then provide information on how to change, such as:

- Discussing it as a social concept
- Telling them where to find clothes
- Discussing the iconography of accessories
- Deciding if staying a newbie is a choice or whether remaining with the stigmatised identity is just too troublesome

It is interesting that even people who have been using Second Life for six months or more can still have newbie status because they have not got to grips with moving, changing/making clothes and becoming familiar with the environment.

### Discuss voice versus text chat

There are still mixed views about the use of text chat versus voice in sessions. For example, some staff prefer text chat because they believe it helps to maintain the sense of immersion of Second Life which they feel voice interrupts. There are an increasing number of research projects exploring this (see for example Carr, 2010), but it is definitely worth discussing with students to seek their views.

## Debate the informal rules of Second Life

Although most people follow the formal rules, there are many other rules that are seen as being rules of courtesy, for example:

- Dressing correctly for the context
- Using the avatar name rather than the person's real name if you know them in real life
- Not using instant messaging for lots of informal conversation during a seminar
- Using the first name of the avatar when addressing them, for example I am 'Second Wind', known as 'Second'
- Remembering that Second Life is not just a game with lots of rules and targets, but is a space that is shaped by its membership
- Using appropriate text speech, pre-agreed with the group.

### Encourage early familiarity with the environment

Encourage students to meet inworld in the first two weeks of the course before they use Second Life for learning sessions, so that they are familiar with the medium.

Staff need to help students to gain confidence in the environment and one of the ways we can do this is by encouraging them to see the learning as contextual and temporal. Students use social cues to work out what and how to learn. Perhaps the success of Second Life in higher education could be argued to be due to the sense of 'eventedness' that occurs in Second Life compared with Discussion Forums. Certainly research into infants has found that they learn more readily when an event is produced by a person rather than an inanimate device (Meltzoff, 1995; 2007). Meltzoff argues:

> Social factors also play a role in lifelong learning—new social technologies (for example, text messaging, Facebook, and Twitter) tap humans' drive for social communication. Educational technology is increasingly embodying the principles of social interaction in intelligent tutoring systems to enhance student learning.
>
> (Meltzoff et al., 2009: 285)

Learning within and across contexts, using reflection and working in teams can also facilitate the processes of sharing attention which are also important for social interaction in virtual worlds. Sharing attention, normally referred to in infant development, is a necessary skill for many complex, natural forms of learning, including learning based on imitation. In this context it is used to describe the process of concentrating together to learn a given task in Second Life. Fiona Littleton at the University of Edinburgh experimented with inducting students into Second Life as individuals and as groups. She found group induction was more effective and less time consuming for the tutors. Sharing a tutor's attention over an induction event offers students common grounds for communication, inworld community building and developing collaborative learning strategies.

### Provide extra training sessions

For some students becoming familiar with Second Life seems almost intuitive – although many staff would argue that Second Life is not a particularly intuitively designed environment. Yet for other students, just moving around is something they find difficult. Providing optional training sessions to practise the basics, even just two one-hour sessions will help to develop student confidence and thereby improve their inworld learning experiences.

## Early activities that work

It is helpful to create activities for students that provide them with a social role to increase their understanding and sense of belonging in Second Life. Activities that are useful include:

- Doing a treasure hunt
- Radically changing appearance
- Changing their walks
- Locating and trying out dance moves
- Taking snapshots to send to one another
- Creating an alternative avatar
- Using interactive activities and demonstrations (see Chapter 8 for a discussion of activities developed by Callaghan et al. (2009) using the Sloodle Tracker)

These kinds of activities help students to come to an understanding of the virtual reality within which they are learning, and therefore enables them to begin the process of secondary socialisation. However, it is advantageous if they can also discuss the processes from real life (their primary space of socialisation) which will and will not work in Second Life. For example, students often make incorrect assumptions based on real life experience, such as assuming they must search for something as in gaming, or that it does not matter what you wear in a tutorial.

## Anticipating problems

### Acknowledge the challenge of inworld identity

It is essential to acknowledge that stripping away real world identity can be unsettling and seen as a loss to some students – the sense of losing one's name, adopting a different appearance and moving differently is often more than uncanny, it is more akin to the numinous than any kind of disjunction. The numinous includes the sense of awe, fear, dread and the uncanny:

> . . . the Numinous is already contained in the idea of the dangerous, or that any perception of danger or any dislike of the wounds and death which it may entail could give the slightest conception of ghostly dread or numinous awe to an intelligence which did not already understand them. When man (*sic*) passes from physical fear to dread and awe, make a sheer jump . . .
>
> (Lewis, 1940: 9)

The idea that students' experiences of Second Life are strongly located in the numinous emerges because of their sense of awe and dread along with sometimes a sense of dual consciousness. Certainly the relationship between the real and the virtual body is something that Sinclair has found troublesome. She asserts:

> The notion of what presence and embodiment mean in digital spaces was something that was constantly problematic for us. The way we seemed to cope in this silent space in the earlier stages of the course was to (super)impose what we 'knew' using an identity we felt we 'had'. We both intuitively felt that this new learning space was distinctively different but it might be that we were imposing difference on it because it was new and unfamiliar, which would seem to be a contestable position, just as is the notion that we are somehow disembodied in cyberspace. Thus, there is an assumption that because we were not 'seeing' non-verbal cues such as eye contact and body language, this is making online learning and communication difficult. However, it might be the case that new and diverse forms of communication are emerging that are creating new textual and identity formulations, not previously located or understood, as Sinclair reflected:

But I don't want to make the separation between the worlds as strongly as yesterday's blog suggests. I always get annoyed when people contrast university with the 'real' world: though I suppose that does fit with students saying it feels like another planet. (I do think that these are two different issues though.) Some of the current discussions and next week's reading are making some very interesting points about what's visible and available and the relationships between online and embodied identities. Yesterday I wrote in my journal, 'I'm not convinced that the embodied identity can be ditched so easily' and left myself an instruction to think about this.

(Savin-Baden and Sinclair, 2010)

### Provide opportunities to discuss difficulties

One of the areas that students find helpful is the opportunity to share barriers and difficulties experienced – not in a way that is so negative that they become despondent, but quite often in terms of feeling somewhat disconcerted. This can take place inworld, through discussion forums and face to face. For example, Gemma, a PhD student studying Second Life explained, 'my worst experience was definitely when someone set off a gun scenario on Coventry island – I know my avatar can't be injured in any way at all, but I found it very unsettling to have someone shooting at me and not know how to defend myself or to shoot back'. Areas to explore with students then might include:

- Student disjunction – getting stuck, feeling frustrated and fragmented
- If and when Lurking occurs in collaborative Second Life learning groups
- How to manage silence and humour
- What to do about over engagement in the learning by becoming over involved in some areas of the course to the detriment of others.

## Managing stuckness

Although the numinous is strongly experienced initially by students, particularly newbies, there is often an ongoing experience of getting stuck in Second Life. One of the areas many staff and students have spoken of in relation to Second Life is something I have come to refer to as *identity stuckness*. This captures the idea that moving learning into immersive virtual worlds introduces a number of issues for students about identity in diverse ways, such as:

## Learner identity

Learner identity expresses the idea that the interaction of learner and learning, in whatever framework, formulates a particular kind of identity. It moves beyond, but encapsulates the notion of learning style, and encompasses positions which students take up in learning situations, whether consciously or unconsciously. Bernstein (1992) suggested that students are in the process of identity formation and that this process may be seen as the construction of pedagogic identities, which will change according to the different relationships that occur between society, higher education and knowledge. Pedagogic identities are defined as those that 'arise out of contemporary culture and technological change that emerge from dislocations, moral, cultural, economic and are perceived as the means of regulating and effecting change' (Bernstein, 1992: 3). Pedagogic identities are seen to be those that arise out of contemporary culture and technological change, while learner identities emerge from the process through which students seek to transcend subjects and disciplines, and the structures embedded in higher education.

## Alternative identities

There has been an increasing tendency to use ALT ('alt' ernative) avatars. It is possible simply to create a new avatar using the same email address but in general you cannot create more than a few accounts in a day using the same email address. The reasons for adopting an ALT avatar often seem to be related to identity play, but can also occur either because people do not want to be disturbed by others (for example tutors by students), or because it is a convenient way to let newbies explore Second Life with one of your ALTs. Warburton suggests:

> The struggle to stabilise the tensions between multiple modes of existence within a single frame can lead to the spawning of a second avatar – a blank persona that can act as a safety valve allowing these multiple states to co-exist. Multiple avatars in effect offer multiple channels for reflecting the range of roles and identities that we take for granted in our everyday existence. This can be a liberating experience for many as it suddenly frees the creator from the behavioural pressures that dominate formal settings even when they are translated into our virtual and imaginary worlds. Multiple avatars also form part of a strategy for addressing

digital reputation management issues that are currently underexposed but of increasing importance to those of us who live and work in virtual spaces.

(Warburton, 2008)

However, for students it is not yet clear how those who have created ALT avatars early in their experience of using Second Life have dealt with these – or whether indeed the tendency to create them is more common amongst experienced Second Life users. Whatever the case, it is something that does seem to raise identities confusion and degrees of stuckness for individuals.

### Identity interruptions

Identity interruptions occur in a number of different ways but the most common is when meeting someone you know reasonably well from real life in Second Life. The experience is often somewhat disarming, but perhaps more so is the realisation that you are responding to them differently because they are manifest in a different way, i.e. as an avatar.

### Identity dressing

There are many varied discussions about dressing, style and hair in Second Life. Yet discussions about appearance that might initially seem superficial may reflect, or begin to reflect, deeper concerns. These might include power relationships between staff and students, but one of the most common ones is that of competiveness within a cohort – over, for example who 'looks the best' or walks with the best walks. However, such discussions may prompt in-depth conversations about identity theft, racism and diversity in Second Life.

## Second Life liminalities

Getting stuck in learning remains an area that is relatively under discussed and under researched. Yet engaging with stuck places – as work by Meyer, Land and others indicates (Land et al., 2008), is central to student, and often staff, learning. This section is my critical reflection based on work in this area by other researchers, rather than research evidence *per se*. As a synthesis of such work, what it does seem to indicate is the need to be aware of the kinds of stuckness that can occur, the ways different types affect students and how staff can recognise it, so that they can then help students effectively. Thus what is presented here draws on the threshold concepts literature, and would seem to have resonance with student experiences of Second Life.

When talking with staff and students, both formally and informally it is clear that they not only experience liminality – the sense of working and learning in betwixt and between spaces, but also experience variations in liminality as defined by Meyer and Land (2006). In the threshold concepts literature the argument is that following a period of being 'stuck', prompted by the threshold concept, one passes through a portal into a space beyond the threshold. They suggest there are four progressive steps towards and through the portal, namely:

- Subliminal variation – variation in students' ways of knowing and understanding the underlying game of the discipline
- Preliminal variation – variation in how students perceive or encounter the portal
- Liminal variation – difference in the way in which the liminal space is entered and negotiated
- Postliminal variation – difference in ways of moving out of the liminal space and into a new terrain

(Paraphrased from Meyer and Land, 2006: 68)

Yet there are also forms of liminality that can be seen in different studies in the field of threshold concepts that might have some application to Second Life. In Meyer et al. (2008) a number of chapters define liminality in particular ways and here I offer exemplars drawn from this work that would seem to be applicable to students' voices:

## Resistance and rupture

The experience of resistance and rupture appears to be a much more troublesome and damaging move into a liminal space than the sense of retreat I have spoken of elsewhere. In retreat (Savin-Baden, 2006) there is a sense of choice, of choosing not to engage with the stuckness because of wanting to avoid engaging with the struggles connected with disjunction and often retreating behind some form of excuse, which means that students do not engage with the personal or organisational catalyst to the disjunction. Whereas resistance and rupture is much more akin to the kind of rupture Heidegger (1985) suggests, whereby it is something that occurs unbidden and is not a product of volition, as retreat often is. Rupture, is as Land suggests:

> Heidegger's 'logic of rupture' and the notion that our practices tend not to be explicit or conspicuous until we encounter some form of rupture (usually through encountering strangeness).

However when we do encounter 'explicitness' in Heidegger's sense (as opposed to our normal 'absorption') there is not, in H.'s view, an automatic process of reflection but often a defensive reaction, or one of inarticulateness or 'speechlessness'.

(Personal communication, June 2008)

This kind of rupture would appear to shift beyond the kinds of variation Meyer et al. (2008) delineate, which suggests that perhaps there are forms or types of liminality that transcend the four variations. This would also appear to be the case in work described by Sibbett and Thompson (2008).

## Moratorium status

Sibbett and Thompson (2008) suggest that in professional development, moratorium status is similar to adolescence where different identity status might be experienced. However, a moratorium status is where delay occurs so that exploration may happen in order to develop, create and form an identity. This, the authors suggest, might be seen as a form of liminality, since by negotiating this process what they term 'identity achievement' (p. 234) occurs. However, if identity work does not take place then it would seem that mimicry may occur, leading to a sense of a fragmentation. This fragmentation seems to happen in many curricula that are educating students though Second Life, and certainly there is evidence for this in the stories of student experience (Savin-Baden and Tombs, 2010).

## Benumbed

In some forms of liminal engagement, probably in the preliminal or subliminal phases, the attempt to avoid or retreat – because of the realisation of not wanting to be in liminal space – results in a sense of being benumbed. Being benumbed also appears to result in a deep stuckness, so there is feeling of not merely a moment of aporia, but of being stuck in the stuckness, so that students are located in a passage of time and space, where the sense of connectedness with anything feels fractal and so disconcerting that crossing over the border into a subliminal space feels and seems impossible. This seems to be particularly evident in those completing large scale project work in Second Life, where just before the final threshold students move into such a state of stuckness that they become inert and want to jettison the whole project.

## Disenchantment

It would seem that in the learning process many students fail to locate the episteme, or underlying game, and this seems particularly apparent in learning in Second Life. Staff attempts to communicate the underlying game have taken a number of forms. For example, there remains a strong focus in higher education and particularly in professional education on the notion of scaffolding learning. Emerging from Vygotsky's zone of proximal development (Vygotsky, 1978), it is the distance between the actual developmental level as determined by independent problem-solving and the level of potential development as determined through problem-solving under adult guidance or in collaboration with more capable peers. The concept of scaffolding refers to the context provided by knowledgeable people to help students develop their cognitive skills. It would seem that staff's need to scaffold learning is troublesome and results in student disenchantment. There is surely the somewhat hegemonic assumption here that teachers' pedagogical stances are better than those held by their students. Indeed, surely to scaffold is to impose one's own pedagogical signature on the way knowledge is created and managed, instead of enabling and allowing students to use or create their own pedagogical signature.

## Conceptually lost

A further type of liminality would seem to be that delineated by Trafford (2008). Trafford explored threshold concepts in PhD supervision and offers some fascinating insights into threshold encounters. What is poignant is the consistent sense of conceptual lostness that students experience, as if they were slipping in and out of liminal variation and across diverse forms of liminality. This sense of being lost and looking for something seems a shift away from liminal variation. This is a response to both preliminal variation in terms of encountering the portal, and liminal variation in terms of how the liminal space is entered and negotiated. Yet it would seem that here students speak of the realisation of being lost and needing to look for something that is there, or having an expectation that this sense of lostness will disappear. Here students seem to almost value doubt as a means of moving away from a liminal space. Instead of trying to eliminate the lostness, they appear to believe it is better to value it as a central principle of learning.

However, much of this is likely to relate to students' long term experience of working in Second Life, while the section below details memories of earlier encounters with Second Life. Many students do enjoy engaging with the Second Life as a learning space but their initial encounters are often troublesome, as demonstrated below.

# Students' perspectives

I asked a few students in Second Life, one who had been in since 2006, the others fairly new (2009), questions about their early experiences. These are presented in Table 7.3.

**Table 7.3**  Students' perspectives

**Things you wished someone had told you about learning in SL?**
How to react to someone if you don't know whether you 'really' know them or not.
How to react to inappropriate behaviour.
How isolated SL is most of the time. However, sometimes that also suited me, too.
I rather wish someone had advised me to find a private space before attempting to change clothes as I'm pretty certain I ended up looking stupid fairly often!
How to manipulate the camera properly – it would have made the world of difference to my early explorations. SL can be very frustrating when you're trying to get your avatar to look at something in just the right way, and it's much much easier if you know how to work the camera functions!
That there's a perceived stigma attached to not customising your clothes or experimenting in that way.

**What was / were the worst mistakes you made?**
Everything that I've done in SL that has been 'wrong', like making myself bald or taking all my clothes off or accidentally deleting an object I've spent ages building, has been a learning experience.
Not just trying things out.
Worrying too much about breaking conventions or being awkward.

**What were your top experiences, and why?**
Finding a community within and around SL which seems to be both happy to share ideas and to support each other.
Being transported to interesting/beautiful places.
Probably when I first figured out how to build something properly - when I first realised that I could manipulate the environment and come to use it in the way that people who are far more familiar with it do.
Being challenged about some real world attitudes.
Teleporting.

# Next steps: designing with students

Having equipped students to dress, use the camera, build and learn in Second Life, it is advantageous to get them involved in the curriculum. This seems a very unusual step, since largely students do not get involved in pedagogic design, but it is an aspect worth exploring. This is because many of the students who become involved in courses that use Second Life will spend time (often more than tutors) exploring areas inworld and invariably will have interesting perspectives on how this media can be used better or differently.

One of the advantages of encouraging students to design activities for other students is that it helps them to consider how to understand and orchestrate learning in Second Life. Students consequently learn how to question knowledge and knowledge construction and reflect on how best to use this media for learning rather than for just conveying content. Helping students to design activities will therefore enable them to:

- Learn about pedagogic design
- Understand Second Life as a medium for learning
- Question and critique what counts as knowledge
- Build a knowledge base that will enable them to critique what counts as learning within their discipline
- Become aware of their own skills and capabilities, and develop confidence in their own critical faculties
- Own the learning and the activities they create
- Become more engaged in learning than something that is tutor designed and tutor-led.

The kinds of activities that students can be encouraged to design therefore might include:

- An orientation activity for newbies
- A workshop on how to teach staff about Second Life
- A learning activity they wished they had been given
- A workshop on building for students in a different discipline from their own.

These are fairly straightforward but ones that students are likely to enjoy designing and, where possible, implementing. However, it is also possible to undertake more substantial curriculum involvement, as suggested by Bovill et al. (2009). As Bovill et al. point out, recent literature has pointed up the need to increase student involvement in curriculum design, since it is evident that active student participation (ASP) in curriculum design both enhances and supports their learning. Yet it is clear from both Bovill et al.'s work and other studies in this area (for example, Nicol, 2008; Reynolds et al., 2004), that issues such as reflexivity, flexibility and the management of power dynamics are ones that need to be considered in-depth by staff who work with students to undertake such a project. Such co-creation can result in greater clarity of learning, teaching and assessment purposes (for staff and students), yet it could also be argued that:

Questions might be raised as to whether the current higher education context is supportive of ASP in curriculum design. The
implied shifts in power and control between tutor and student
would require a university which encourages students to act critically and to challenge and question the world in which they
live (Barnett, 1997; Haggis, 2006). Yet, many authors have raised
concerns that universities are losing their criticality in the face of
the recent surge of managerialism and instrumentalism in the UK
higher education sector. They suggest that this vision of a critical
higher education may be under threat (Barnett and Coate, 2005;
Rice, 2004; Taylor et al., 2002; Barnett, 1997).

(Bovill et al., 2009: 24)

However, as Second Life media is relatively new to higher education I
would suggest that co-creation can be helpful to students, staff, the institution and higher education in general. What is perhaps pertinent is how
such design might be implemented, beyond the development of small
scale activities as suggested above. Yet perhaps some possibilities might
include

- Students receiving credit or remuneration for designing a module
- Participatory evaluation undertaken by students throughout the
  life of a course or module which they are undertaking
- Designing two or three activities within a module with an opportunity to run and receive credit for organising those sessions.

## Conclusion

This chapter has considered a range of issues including ways of helping
students to manage stuckness and liminality, along with ways of enabling
them to become co-creators in Second Life design. What is important too
is that we acknowledge that many students will have greater technological range and capability than many staff in higher education, and this
needs to be harnessed. Yet equipping students for learning in Second Life
also requires that assessment processes and practices are aligned in ways
that support teaching and enhance students' learning. Although there are
many debates about the purposes and types of assessment in higher education, the next chapter will suggest that the adoption of Second Life
can encourage a reconsideration of assessment issues, in order that assessments are designed to support student learning and development rather
than just to test knowledge.

# 8    Assessment for learning
#      in Second Life

## Introduction

The literature on assessment of learning in Second Life is somewhat sparse and this chapter suggests that the issue of assessment in Second Life differs little from concerns about assessment in higher education in general. This provides exemplars of assessment that fit effectively with the notion of assessment *for* learning in Second Life. It begins by exploring assessment practices in general and suggests that there is a need to move away from striated assessment practices towards smooth ones along with sound feedback mechanisms. The latter section presents, as well as recommends, forms of assessment that are being used in Second Life, some of which meet the idea of smooth assessment more readily than others.

## How will the learning be assessed?

Assessment in Second Life does not differ from concerns about assessment in higher education in general, because the learning that occurs in Second Life is part of a programme or module and therefore assessment in Second Life cannot be separated from the rest of the course. The work of Deleuze and Guattari is helpful in examining assessment, since they argue for smooth and striated cultural spaces (Deleuze and Guattari, 1988: 478). For them the notion of smooth space is one of becoming, it is a nomadic space where the movement is more important than the arrival. By contrast in a striated space, the focal point is one of arrival, arrival at the point towards which one is oriented. In general, university assessment tends to be striated – assessment is characterised by a strong sense of organisation and boundedness. Assessment is bounded not only through the traditions of the discipline and the signature pedagogies, but also by university structures and procedures. Such striated systems mean that learning spaces are diminished, and personal engagement with such spaces is often demeaned by others. The aim of this approach is to use assessment to regulate, control and promote learning using the 'stick' of grades. It is about regulating how much students study, what they study and the quality of their engagement. Yet if there is to be a shift toward smooth assessment, where teachers seek to respond to student work, make judgments about what counts as good learning and what strategies might help improve the work (I discuss this in more depth later in the chapter), it is important to focus on

- When is assessment to occur?
- Who is being assessed?
- Who is going to carry out the assessment?
- What method of assessment will be used?
- How is grading/marking to be done?
- What feedback will students receive?

Hounsell et al. (2007) raise a number of thought provoking ideas related to the concept of assessment and the notion that there needs to be some balance in the use of assessment in our educational institutions. The implication is that, for the most part, assessment is not being used well to achieve the aims of educating our students, and this would seem particularly to be the case with learning in Second Life. Some of the reasons described include:

- The purpose of the given assessment has not been clearly identified by the teacher and therefore the task set does not achieve its purpose. Is it formative or summative?
- There is disjunction between the learning intentions of the course and what is being assessed in the course. For example, are all the learning outcomes being equally assessed? Should they be equally assessed or are some learning outcomes more important than others? Are all outcomes being assessed or are a few of them being repeatedly assessed and others not assessed at all? Is it important for the type of assessment to reflect the way in which students are learning in the class and what activities are being valued in the class, if we want students to consolidate their learning?
- The fractionalisation of assessment tasks so that in reality there are many small tasks that contribute a small grade toward the overall course grade. The underlying reasoning here is that students do not value a piece of work unless it is graded; that they are only motivated by grades and not the intrinsic learning value of each task.

## Assessment or grading?

It has become commonplace to hear lecturers claim that students will not do any work unless it is being assessed – by which they often mean graded.

However, as Knight notes (2001), assessment for summative purposes is seen as being so important that those being assessed see it as being in their own interests both to play up what they do know or can do and to cover up as much as possible what they do not know or cannot do – however little and badly. Knight (2001) examines some of the problems with grading, not least if a norm-referenced approach is adopted. It is also worth asking why we are giving marks other than to aggregate them in a somewhat dubious process to arrive at degree classifications. Knight's section on the four assessment concepts of reliability, validity, affordability and usability are also particularly pertinent. For example, in saying that for assessment to be reliable we expect it to be objective, accurate, repeatable and analytically sound:

> Although these routines might produce 'objective' data, they often fail, say their critics, to reflect the complexity of human achievements
>
> (p. 11)

Further:

> The need for reliability pushes us towards certainty and simplicity but modern higher education curricula value complex, fuzzy achievements exemplified by soft skills, autonomy, creativity, incremental self-theories, interpersonal fluency, etc.
>
> (p. 13)

Woods, who used problem-based learning in his Chemical Engineering courses at McMaster University in Canada, defines assessment as 'a judgement based on the degree to which the goals have been achieved based on measurable criteria and on pertinent evidence' (Woods, 2000: 21). He contends that the definition can be best applied by breaking it down into five principles:

1) Assessment is a judgement based on performance – not personalities.
2) Assessment is a judgement based on evidence, not feelings – whatever our intuition about a student's abilities, we need evidence.
3) Assessment should be done for a purpose with clearly defined performance conditions.
4) Assessment is a judgement done in the context of published goals, measurable criteria and pertinent, agreed-upon forms of evidence.
5) Assessment should be based on multidimensional evidence: static and dynamic situations; small assignments and lengthy projects; academic, social and personal contexts; under a variety of

performance conditions; formative and summative data and with different persons being the assessors.

## Reviewing assessment

The effectiveness of learning in Second Life depends largely upon matching the needs of a particular learner or group of learners to the information available. It is important to ensure that assessment is aligned with the module objectives and the learning and teaching approach adopted, in this case problem-based learning. It is equally important to ask why the assessment is being done. For example, it could be to:

- Support and improve learning (formative assessment)
- Measure learning and provide certification (summative assessment)
- Assure standards (summative assessment).

It is important to find mechanisms for placing information in a learning context, and then to exploit the student response. Systems designed to create feedback based on counters that link directly to student decision-making (Conradi et al., 2009) can be extended and adapted to provide reporting systems, which allow both scenario evaluation and simple formative and summative student assessments.

Although as yet there is relatively little written about assessment in Second Life, there is a body of literature on e-assessment. For example, the JISC report Effective Practice with e-Assessment provides relatively little delineation of what may be considered e-assessment and if indeed it was actually any different from other assessment issues. Further, the report seems to have a strong focus on the kinds of assessment that focussed on 'right answers' and were highly teacher and test centred. Perhaps assessment needs to be relocated and considered in terms of new values *rather* than assessment practices that value:

1) gaps that can be fixed
2) performance over learning
3) the information we give the students rather than information they give to us
4) assessment practices that confirm our teaching beliefs
5) assessment and feedback which helps to improve teaching (or helps us to teach to the test better, even if we deny this).

Many of the debates to date relating to assessment for learning focus on approaches that ensure that students fit the model. Thus any notions of the student having a voice or stance toward knowledge is located in students being expected to conform to and work within the standards set by staff, which then necessarily implies there is not only a right way to learn, but also a right way to respond to the assessment. Thus assessment such as this is striated; it is characterised by a strong sense of organisation and boundedness. Assessment is bounded not only through the traditions of the discipline and the signature pedagogies, but also by university structures and procedures. Such striated systems mean that learning spaces are diminished, and personal engagement with such spaces is often demeaned by others. The aim of this approach is to use assessment to regulate, control and promote learning using the 'stick' of grades. It is about regulating how much students study, what they study and the quality of their engagement. The overall strategy adopted here rests on 'capturing' sufficient study time by means of summative assessment tasks in order to enable students to achieve the desired goals. The other strategy suggested is to use social pressure, for example students having to give a presentation in front of their peers. To move away from these approaches, which focus on ways of ensuring students' performance can be adopted to fit assessment practices, requires relocating both learning and assessment into 'smooth curriculum spaces' (Savin-Baden, 2007a).

## Smooth assessment practices

It would seem that the most useful way of assessing learning in Second Life is adopting smooth assessment, which is where assessment is seen as an open, flexible and contested space in which both learning and learners are always on the move. Movement is not towards a given trajectory; instead, there is a sense of displacement of notions of time and place, so that assessment for learning is delineated with and through the staff and students; by the creators of the space(s). These kinds of assessment for learning are likely to be seen as risky, since they prompt consideration of what counts as legitimate knowledge. In such assessment for learning, students will be encouraged to examine the underlying structures and belief systems implicit within what is being learned, in order to not only understand the disciplinary area but also its credence. What will be important is that uncertainty and gaps are recognised, along with the realisation of the relative importance of gaps between different knowledge and different knowledge hierarchies. In this approach teachers and learners seek to respond to student work, making judgements about what counts as good learning and what strategies might help to improve the work. Like Rust et al. (2005), those who adopt this stance believe that assessment criteria only make sense when they are being questioned or clarified through dialogue (deconstructed). However, the debate must be seen more widely than the socialisation of students into an accepted way of thinking. Instead, assessment needs to be seen as a discursive social practice in Second

Life, with the acknowledgement that what counts as legitimate knowledge is framed by institutional discourse and boundaries and the demands of summative assessment. This perspective therefore both acknowledges that issues of power are in play and embraces notions of learner identities. Here, then, the pedagogic context becomes the object of the critique, rather than functioning to deliver knowledge. In summary, this active and constructive participation takes the form of reflection which involves:

1) Students bringing their academic work into a relationship with their identities
2) Critique and deconstruction of criteria
3) Developing a 'feel for the game'. Students can take their ideas/ understanding from one context to another
4) Initiating a process of 'motivation', seen here through a socio-cultural lens
5) Encouraging students to negotiate the meaning of assessment, so that they can both discuss and also decide with staff and peers what it means in their own terms for them as individuals.

Smooth assessment then is embodied in classroom interaction, rather than being viewed as a quick fix or adjunct. This is a discursive shift away from knowledge/transmission/acquisition models of learning and convergent models of formative assessment based upon behaviourist approaches, where teachers' feedback reinforces correct answers. Smooth assessment then reflects the values of 'assessment for learning' suggested by authors such as McDowell et al. (2008) and Pryor and Croussard (2007), whereby learning should be seen as a process of 'coming to know in certain situations,' enabling learners to engage with new ways of being and acting associated with new aspirational identities, which are then legitimated. The work by Pryor and Croussard (2007) argues for the use of third spaces between convergent and divergent assessment, along with the need for staff to undertake code switching between different pedagogic repertoires in order to do this. Yet there is a need to move across to formative assessment in order to begin to interrupt and acknowledge disciplinary power and practices, which are not merely imposed through university systems, but are in fact designed and supported by staff values and perspectives about disciplinarity, knowledge and assessment. However, what is essential to smooth assessment is effective feedback.

## Effective feedback

The early literature on feedback largely centred on a deficit model and research has tended to focus on processes for improvement. Certainly when using problem-based learning in Second Life, evidence suggests that students valued fast and informative feedback (for example, Conradi et al., 2009). As Hounsell (2008) has pointed out, what is now needed is promulgation of excellent feedback practices. Part of the current difficulty is perhaps due to a lack of clarity about what counts as feedback, the way in which feedback is located pedagogically and the relationship between feedback pedagogy and feedback practices. Glover and Brown (2006), for example, argue that most students see feedback as written comments on their work. The difficulty with the early teacher-led models of feedback is a sense that assessment feedback is one way, from staff to students, resulting in a kind of assessment monologism. Thus Second Life feedback should be:

- Soundly located pedagogically
- Explored in more depth in relation to discipline-based pedagogy
- Examined extensively in relation to student perceptions, student learning, students' conceptions of the assessment and the impact on grades.

Assessment should also draw on findings from the 80Days project. The 80Days project assessed players' feelings, and emotional and affective responses, by examining different criteria such as immersion, goals, autonomy, feedback, concentration and challenge. The findings from the 80Days project suggest that the following feedback/interventions should be implemented:

1) Skill activation interventions may be applied if a learner gets 'stuck' in some area of the problem space and some skills are not used, although the user model assumes that the user masters these skills.
2) Skill acquisition interventions may be applied in a similar situation, however, the user model assumes that the user does not master the unused skill.
3) Motivational interventions may be applied, for example, if the learner does not act for a certain, expected long time.
4) Assessment clarification interventions may be applied, for example, in the form of a query if the learner's actions give contradicting support for and against the assumption of a certain competence state.

Although numerous studies have been undertaken to explore student perspectives of assessment (for example, Birenbaum, 1997; Boud, 1995; Sambell et al., 1997; Sambell and McDowell, 1998), there have been few studies that have examined and compared assessment in asynchronous threaded discussion and synchronous discussion in immersive worlds.

## Assessments that work with Second Life

There are many programmes that use Second Life but they tend, in the main, not to assess students in their use of Second Life *per se*. Yet assessments do occur which build on learning that takes place in Second Life. Some of these include asking students to:

- design games for learning purposes – games and treasure hunts designed for peers create a sense of flow and fun in learning but more importantly they help students to become familiar with tools in Second Life and are relatively easy to assess.
- undertake a literature review – although this is a useful activity in general and helps students become familiar with the Second Life and virtual worlds literature, it is not really a medium that relates particularly well to learning in Second Life.
- undertake a team-led project – these are very effective but are difficult to mark and you have to decide whether you are marking content, process, building scripting, presentation or all of these.
- analysing a student designed activity using peer assessment. These work well with Second Life and help students to not only understand the assessment process but develop criticality toward their own work. Further, it allows students to think more carefully about what they know, what they do not know, and what they need to know to accomplish certain tasks.

A number of documented assessments, as well as some of my own suggestions, are presented below:

### Quests and quizzes

There are several ways of using quests and they are advantageous because they can quickly show tutors what it is students do and do not understand. Students also receive immediate feedback which helps their learning. An example of a recently developed quiz is that of Bloomfield and Livingstone (2009) who developed 'quizHUD'. This has been developed alongside the SLOODLE project. It allows educators to prepare learning material and quizzes through a web-based interface, and to integrate it with Second Life. The authors argue that:

> Its aim is to harness the benefits of web-based learning and assessment, such as convenience for the student, and objectivity of grading, while incorporating the benefits of virtual worlds, such as immersive navigation
>
> (Bloomfield and Livingstone, 2009: 1)

In practice this device uses a heads-up display in Second Life. Students engage with assessed and non-assessed questions, allowing the tutor to evaluate the students' progress through the material. What is interesting about this assessment is that it provides both a multiple choice quiz with a grade, and also what are termed 'Explore Questions'. Here the information is presented differently, in short instead of seeing a series of answers and clicking a corresponding tab, the student answers by clicking on an object in his or her environment. The difference here is that the students are required to engage with the relevant object and the virtual surroundings. This would seem the kind of assessment then that does not just focus on a surface approach to learning content, but encourages student engagement in the environment and the learning task.

Addison and O'Hare (2008) suggest the value of using quests to assess student role play. In this project a food factory was developed in Second Life to allow regulators to undertake an immersive role play, with students taking on the role of a regulatory officer visiting an unfamiliar factory, to question production staff on a working line, company managers and other members of the workforce. Although this is yet to be implemented, the assessment they suggest is useful and marries well with the teaching approach adopted. Here the assessment requires that students collect an information sheet in the form of a notecard from a dispenser and must decipher the clues it provides which must be collected from scripted objects to complete the chosen quest. The authors suggest that this assessment could be used to assess students' competence:

> For example a clipboard (the scripted object) could be carried by the student, and when they believe that they have found one of the key inspection points then they could be required to click on the point which would provide a tick on their board. This information can be transferred directly to tutors by the participants putting their completed boards into a collection point which notifies the tutor by e-mail.
>
> (Addison and O'Hare, 2008: 14)

### Problem analysis

There are many ways of undertaking problem analysis. It is a complex skill needed in many disciplines but one that can be easily overlooked. Students often attempt to solve problems without first working out what the problem is in the first place. Using problem analysis in Second Life can be useful for developing sound analysis skills. For example, a recent problem analysis was developed for a module in environmental health related to noise pollution. Students were required to go to a housing estate on Coventry University Island and assess noise levels. Having made their assessment and posted their report to the tutor in a drop box, they then attended a course on noise assessment and finally retook the test in Second Life. This meant students were able to compare their progress and receive tutor feedback both on their report and face to face. This kind of test is one that can also be used for distance students.

## Reports

Written communication is another skill important for students. Requiring written reports allows students to practise this form of communication, particularly if the word allowance is short and it can promote succinct, critical pieces of work. The use of team-based reports has been used successfully in the PREVIEW project by paramedic students, who were required to submit their report through a drop box in Second Life and then received feedback within 24 hours from a tutor. This meant they could return and practise the scenario again if they desired, and attempt to improve their performance.

## Machinima-based assessment

The increasing interest and use of machinima in Second Life has also had an impact on assessment. It is a medium that is used in a number of art and design courses that have adopted Second Life. However, a good example is that of Brown et al. (2008) who used machinima assessment by asking students to work in groups to create short video clips from their activities in Second Life. Group assessment is often difficult because asking the students to submit their work orally or in written form as a collaborative piece is difficult to mark. Is content, process, presentation or a combination of these being marked? Brown et al. used the following schema which appeared to work well and can clearly be adapted for use in other disciplines:

> Each group compiled a joint report containing individual reflections on how they approached the following assessment instructions:
> **Common Elements – 40%**
> (one copy, worked on by all in the group), comprising:
> Narrative: the concept and content of what is being shown (image, sound, models)
> Storyboard: with asset list indicating who was the author of each asset.
> Production and editing of video

**Individual artefacts – 40%**
(contribution to the group)
Account of how the Machinima video was made. Description of artefacts made – at least one each of: Bitmap image or texture, vector graphic, 3D Second Life artefact.
Presentation – structure and coherence of document in report format.
**Group Presentation – 20%**
Demonstrate machinima video, supported by a brief explanation of what you have done and be prepared to answer questions on your work

(Brown et al., 2008: 41)

### Team wikis

These work well with Second Life and can also be used successfully in terms of a team writeboard. Team wikis allow multiple users to contribute to a website, essentially web pages that are editable by a number of people. What is also useful about these is that it is possible to assess who has contributed what to the wiki and the collaborative work. However, as in collaborative assessment, it is important to award a team mark so that the team learns to manage the passengers, lurkers and thinkers. Further as Lea (2001) pointed out: collaborative learning is not just about enabling a dialogue between students working together, and pooling their understandings of authoritative published works; it can also be about creating collaborative texts . . . even when the final piece of work is that of an individual student for assessment purposes (Lea, 2001: 178).

However, the challenge of these assessments is that for students it is often difficult to share inchoate work. This kind of assessment also raises issues about:

1) Honesty in the student group and ground rules of sharing, in terms of what belongs to whom
2) Taking time away from the discussion board in order to do wiki work
3) Students' position as author on the wiki and whether, and if so how, they should 'mark' ownership
4) How students changing, improving or ruining other entries affected ownership by authors and therefore the assessment
5) How work will be perceived by staff and peers when much of it is 'work in progress'
6) What counts as knowledges in this space and who decides

7)  Whether the wiki is a less contested space and knowledge is seen as more solid in a wiki compared with a discussion forum

8)  Which postings were changed by students and which were not. For example, were those made by tutors more likely to be added to rather than changed directly because s/he was contributing to a student's assignment space?

## Blogs

Weblogs have become a popular web-publishing form in the last two or three years, and are perhaps best described as web-based diaries used by students for online reflection, a space/place to bring together reflections, thoughts and ideas. Blogs are invariably assessed on issues such as:

- *Reflection*: the extent to which the blog illustrates criticality and reflection through the period of the course or module.
- *Regularity*: the extent to which blog entries are frequent and substantial, spread throughout the course.
- *Knowledge and understanding*: this section of the blog should demonstrate in-depth understanding of the area under study and the ability to take a critical stance towards the knowledge and perspectives being offered through the course.

## Linked assessments

These kinds of assessment are a series of assessments that relate directly to the learning and encourage students to think across knowledge boundaries. For example, Thackray et al. (2008) used Second Life to teach students about the creation of interactive learning environments, in an option module available to third year undergraduates and Masters. In practice this required students to create an interactive learning experience in Second Life for their clients, to prepare a machinima describing their work, and to prepare three written pieces of work, namely, a project specification, a group description of the process, and an individual, reflective document. All these assignments linked together around one project which varied according to the clients.

## Hypertext essays

These are scholarly works or artefacts that can only be realised electronically and have been written with particular hypertext practices in mind. These include, for example, multilinearity, repetition, mixed media and multivocality. A hypertext essay can be read in many different ways.

McKenna and McAvinia (2007) suggest 'when it comes to analysing hypertext writing, there has been much written by theorists about fiction and professional, published, academic writing...however, there has been rather less said about how student writers are experimenting with academic hypertext'. They suggest that hypertext writing might subvert the dominant forms of meaning making in higher education. Furthermore the students in their study suggested that hypertext writing challenged them to operate within a different form of academic discourse than more traditional forms of essay writing.

## Conclusion

Although there seems to be relatively little relaxation of the coded assessment practices of higher education, what does seem to be evident is that Second Life promotes a greater sense of collegiality than a discussion forum, and such spaces will perhaps enable a redistribution of educational power, so that components of Second Life curricula and assessment become spaces of consultation rather than those of containment and control. It is apparent that assessment needs to be seen as developmental rather than regulatory, and as a practice that enables students to develop and come to an understanding of the literary practices of higher education and the disciplines in which they are studying. As Goodfellow and Lea (2005) point out: we cannot conflate the writing that students do in online discussion only with social or collaborative interaction but that the texts themselves are evidence of the different literacy practices through which students are constructing disciplinary knowledge (Goodfellow and Lea, 2005: 267). Further, Ulmer (2003a, 2003b) suggests that just transferring and transforming literacy onto the Internet in the form of ready-made papers put on websites is not enough. Instead, he suggests that it is vital to create pedagogies that will enable the integration of Internet practices with literate skills in new and innovative ways. Perhaps yet again we need to ask the question: what is assessment for? Then we need to reframe it for a later modern supercomplex world. As so many of the debates about learner and learner centred-ness take the stance that learning *is* conceptualised as a process whereby students actively construct their own knowledge (Barr and Tagg, 1995), then there are questions to be asked about how staff can assess this without adopting smooth assessment practices. There are a number of other technological developments that have recently emerged, and Chapter 9 presents these, suggesting that some of them might be used to enhance teaching and assessment in Second Life.

# Part 3

## Shifting boundaries

# 9 Harnessing technology for learning

## Introduction

This chapter will focus on new technological developments for enhancing learning. Some of these have been developed specifically for Second Life, whilst obviously others have not, but might be adapted. It begins by presenting projects such as <u>SLOODLE</u> and <u>PIVOTE</u> which have been designed for Second Life use, and have been tested and adapted to improve them following user feedback. The second section of the chapter explores some of the recently funded projects by the European Union, that have possibilities for adaptation to Second Life.

## Repurposing and redesigning

Whilst most staff have become familiar with using virtual learning environments for learning, linking immersive virtual worlds such as Second Life with virtual learning environments remains troublesome. One of the most common complaints is that immersive virtual worlds are platform-based and are unwieldy to use. Yet by repurposing and redesigning them it will be possible to allow for more flexible use and for more diverse purposes in ways that will enhance learning. Browser-based tools will enable the same learning scenario to be used across different media, ranging from mobile phones to high-end computer systems.

Whilst there are other immersive virtual worlds in use (<u>Activeworlds</u>, <u>There</u>) Second Life is currently the most widely used in higher education and with an open source can be adapted to overcome the following current difficulties. What is needed is the creation of semantic virtual worlds which focus not on technology, but on purpose and pedagogy; how teachers might want to use them, and what purpose they will serve. A focus then on purpose and pedagogy would mean:

- Harnessing emotion and immersion for learning, so that learning in IVWs gains some of the advantages of face-to-face learning which is currently lost via managed learning systems such as Blackboard

- Providing flexible social networking – such as using Sparkle on iphones to access immersive virtual worlds
- Providing immersive virtual worlds such as Second Life via a browser, to reduce bandwidth and graphics problems.

To date there are a number of projects that have begun to tackle technology in ways that are designed to enhance learning. Although the ones discussed below do not all use Second Life, they are projects that might be adapted for immersive virtual worlds in the future.

## Second Life integration

There are a number of projects – some more effective and useful than others, that have undertaken the task of linking Second Life with other forms of learning in order to make the student experience more coherent. Below are four projects which seem to be attracting growing interest and having an impact:

### SLOODLE (Simulation Linked Object Oriented Dynamic Learning Environment)

This aims to bring together Second Life and the virtual learning environment Moodle and has undergone a number of iterations. The original idea was to create a 3D course in Moodle through which it would be possible to map course content pages onto objects in Second Life. However, the project became more extensive and developed into three main areas: the product of SLOODLE as software; the SLOODLE community, a group of users and developers; and the research studies related to SLOODLE for academic and product development. Initially some of the difficulties experienced were that SLOODLE software was not sufficiently easy to install, but since then new versions have been released. This is a development that looks certain to progress in some disciplines and as Kemp et al. argue:

> We believe that 3D settings open a broad landscape for exploration in distance education and blended learning, especially when connected to mature VLE technologies. Combining a 3D environment with a VLE allows for verifiable identity management, integrated support for assessment and proven structures for student collaboration and reflection. SLOODLE is still a young project and only a relatively small core set of features have been developed.
>
> (Kemp et al., 2009: 554)

There does seem to be a move away from SLOODLE in some areas, with some universities starting to move towards more browser based and mobile solutions. Furthermore Second Life <u>Viewer 2</u> poses an interesting challenge to SLOODLE as in theory you should now be able to access Moodle from inside Second Life without SLOODLE. Yet at the same time those in computer science and engineering do seem to be adapting it for other means:

### SLOODLE tracker

The SLOODLE tracker is an extension created at the University of Ulster for recording and archiving user interactions inside virtual worlds. The potential opportunities this extension could provide are presented by Callaghan et al.:

> The extensive course management tools available in Moodle do not currently exist in most virtual worlds whose main strength in this context is the provision of immersive spaces for social interaction and experiential based learning (Slator et al., 2004). However, this does raise one major concern in the use of virtual worlds for education in that while they offer the ability to freely explore open worlds, they can lack a top down narrative and a formal structure with explicit user objectives and learning outcomes (Mason and Moutahir, 2006). These current deficiencies could hamper the widespread adoption of virtual worlds as a tool for technology enhanced learning. The need for functionality which integrates virtual worlds with the established institutional virtual learning environments to share data with existing academic information systems is essential.
>
> (Callaghan et al., 2009)

The idea behind the SLOODLE tracker is that students' interaction with objects, simulations and activities alone or in teams on a Second Life island can be tracked and recorded. Although this seems very outcomes based and quantitative, what it does do is ensure that students are engaging with the activities. It also indicates to staff where students' learning difficulties are likely to be. Once completed, the tracker enables staff and students to review the actions as they are automatically recorded in Moodle.

### PIVOTE

PIVOTE is a virtual learning authoring system for virtual worlds. It was developed as part of the <u>JISC</u> funded <u>PREVIEW</u> project. PIVOTE is based on the Medbiquitous Virtual Patient standard, and the system can be used for any sort of structured learning in virtual worlds. The key point about PIVOTE is that all the structure and information content of an exercise is stored on the web, not in the virtual world. This means that it is easy to create, and then edit and maintain, courseware independent of the virtual worlds. As structure and content are separate it is possible to reuse the same scenarios, adapting them for different courses and levels. It is currently focussed on how you manage the user task, rather than the environment, yet work by Nabil Asif is seeking to make this more accessible and easy to use for teachers. The Medbiquitous Virtual Patient model on which PIVOTE is based comprises a branched architecture based on learner options, rather than teacher or automated changes to adapt the environment. Daden have begun to introduce the concept of teacher initiated actions, and how the scope can be extended. This will allow PIVOTE to support a library of responses to various adaptation triggers, managing these alongside, but separate from, the learner activity flow.

It is possible to download all the code you need to use PIVOTE to run your own courses in virtual worlds. From the PIVOTE Information Centre in Second Life you can download a starter set of objects, and the Controller, and then create and share your own. Resources for PIVOTE:

- Watch video tutorials on YouTube
- Download an Introduction to PIVOTE (PDF) or PIVOTE Overview (PDF slideshow), and other documentation from our Google Code site.

## SLAVE

This technology was developed at the University of Malta by Camilleri and Montebello to create an environment in Second Life inhabited by 'intelligent assistants', essentially chatbots. The chatbots guide students and help them to learn. The underlying premise of the project was that Second Life often seemed empty and that students were not able to undertake activities inworld without the presence of the tutor. Examples within the project include a chess game with a chatbot and the 'search sculpty' that listens on chat channel 0 'for a particular command concatenated with a string and searches the Wikipedia for such a string'. However, perhaps the most helpful activity is the use of a Pandora bit to guide students on their journey through Second Life.

The advantages of SLAVE are the opportunities it provides for students to practise and explore new media and Second Life spaces. However, the authors suggest:

The weaknesses of SLAVE lie in the lack of direction and the complexity involved in using multiple modalities to explain concepts. The lack of pedagogic learning agents on the virtual world doesn't reinforce connectivism in learning and learners on SLAVE didn't have the necessary networking platform to share experiences and resources with peers.

(Camilleri and Montebello, 2008)

However, it would seem that this is a project with some interesting developments that would bear further work, and could be reused and adopted across a number of disciplines.

There are many other emerging developments such as the use of haptics in Second Life for visually impaired people (de Pascale et al., 2008). This project sought to design two new inputs modes that have used the force-feedback capabilities of haptic devices to enable the use of Second Life for blind people. The design was tested with people who were blindfolded but the authors suggest that they found it possible to detect other avatars and were able to perform tasks.

## Projects that might be adapted for Second Life use

One of the difficulties with implementing any innovation is that critics will argue it offers nothing new or is just a gimmick. Perhaps some of the recent innovations have not helped this situation, as studies such as ICOPER have sought to classify teaching methods in ways that imply that learning and teaching can be delineated, ordered and contained. ICOPER, a study funded by the European Commission, examined exchange of competency models and learning outcomes, collaboration around learning designs, and the reuse of instructional models and content in learning delivery environments. Whilst the project team argue they are adopting a user-led approach, the initial explorations and modelling have been author-led, with few higher education pedagogical models being used to inform these. It is an interesting project but seems not to draw on the considerable wealth of early taxonomies available and suggests that the classification of generalised teaching methods will be helpful to improve learning, which earlier pedagogical studies have shown not to be the case.

Projects such as ICOPER seem to deny the fluidity of learning and seek to define, narrow and position learning in ways that deny the value of ubiquitous social networking, and the desirability of focusing learning (not teaching). They do not see the value of bringing students in as co-producers of knowledge rather than merely end users of it. The ICOPER project is just one of many examples that raises questions about how useful it is to classify teaching methods, introduces queries about how such teaching methods relate to approaches for learning and educational theory, and perhaps more pertinently whether in fact it is useful to classify teaching methods decontextualised from the discipline in which they are being used. A further difficulty is that although some recent studies have sought to focus on teaching when designing technical solutions, there remain many difficulties. However, there are projects that may be adapted:

The projects <u>XDELIA</u> ((E)Xcellence in Decision making through Enhanced Learning in Immersive Applications) and <u>COSPATIAL</u> (Communication and Social Participation: collaborative Technologies for Interaction and Learning) seek to support the transfer and generalisation of skills acquired during specific tested tasks and to mimic important aspects of real-life situations, with the aim of improving the possibility of transferring acquired competencies to practice. A further project, namely <u>eCIRCUS</u> (Education Through Characters With Emotional-Intelligence And Role-playing Capabilities That Understand Social Interaction) used virtual role play with characters that established relationships with the learner. eCIRCUS had many pedagogical similarities with problem-based learning, as it sought to develop models of narrative engagement and empathy in order to investigate and understand cognitive, social and emotional learning processes through role play.

<u>COOPER</u> (Collaborative Open Environment for Project-Centred Learning) has developed and tested a model-driven extensible environment that supports distance-learners in virtual teams working together in projects to solve complex problems. In COOPER, the focus is on knowledge management for teams and it is predominantly a Learning Management System. Further similarities, such as pedagogical scenarios, distance learners, collaborative teams etc., can also be observed. Both COOPER and COSPATIAL rely on information processing models of teaching, whereby memory may be episodic, involving recall of events in detail and sequence, or it may be semantic, involving encoding, storage and retrieval of information. According to information processing theorists, a number of factors can affect rote learning, such as meaningfulness, placement of an item within a list, practice or rehearsal, transfer or interference of prior learning, organisation (chunking or categorising), encoding, context and mnemonics. Cognitive theorists seek to understand how individuals learn and what goes on inside the mind when learning occurs. This kind of education focuses on cognitive structuring, which is essential for developing capacity and skills for improving learning, or learning how to learn.

Although earlier work in face-to-face studies (for example Eva et al., 1998) has suggested that transfer between contexts can be problematic, it increasingly seems that practising skills improves transfer. Recent research on virtual reality and simulations would seem to suggest that transfer is more likely from virtual situations to real life situations than early work on transfer across different real world settings had previously implied. For example, the level of motivation to learn that immersion provides is also important. Dede (1995) argues that the capacity to shape and interact with the environment is highly motivating and sharply focuses attention. Similarly Warburton (2009) indicates that the immersive nature of the virtual world can provide a compelling educational experience, particularly in relation to simulation and role-playing activities. Herrington et al. (2003) refer to the authenticity of the virtual settings, arguing that they have the capability to motivate and encourage learner participation by facilitating students' willing suspension of disbelief.

An e-commerce perspective has been taken by Chittaro and Ranon (2000) who developed a means of allowing the customer to interact with the e-commerce service through a 3D representation of a store which enabled users to look around and pick up products from shelves. Recently, they also applied their techniques to e-learning (Chittaro and Ranon, 2007, 2008) by creating Adaptive EVE which is an e-learning platform tailored to the knowledge level of the learners and to their preferred learning style. Unfortunately it does not provide an authoring tool that allows the author to easily specify an adaptive environment. None of these approaches consider collaborative learning in terms of how these technological innovations might enhance learning in and though groups nor do they examine the learning context or the emotions of learners. However, a study by Benford et al. (1995) explored user embodiment on collaborative virtual environments. The purpose of the study was to provide users with what researchers considered to be appropriate representative body images. The underlying argument here is that if given real life bodies provide continuous information, feedback and means of communication, then embodiment in virtual environments should be the same, so that participants can represent themselves as accurately as possible. The authors suggest the following list: presence, location, identity, activity, availability, history of activity, viewpoint, actionpoint, gesture, facial expression, voluntary versus involuntary expression, degree of presence, capabilities, physical properties, manipulating one's view of others, multiple media, distributed bodies, truthfulness and efficiency. Whilst this is an interesting study and suggested framework, it currently seems unclear as to whether such a framework will increase the sense of embodiment. The extent to which there is difference between designed embodiments such as this, and the use of other digital media such as Skype is also unclear, as is whether in fact embodiment is seen as more realistic the more representative it is of real life compared with user designed avatars in spaces such as Second Life. Perhaps this is also all linked to broader issues such as immersion and emotion.

An authoring tool that does allow authors to create their own virtual reality adaptive course has been developed in the context of the GRAPPLE project (De Troyer et al., 2009). The GRAPPLE project mainly focuses on classical learning material, but adaptation of virtual reality and simulation is also considered. However, once again it is not in the context of collaborative learning or considering the emotions of the learners. Another closely related field where adaptivity has been considered is that of educational games. Moreno-Ger et al. (2008a) have developed an approach called <e-Adventure>, which is an educational game engine that supports an adaptive model. The <e-Adventure> platform also includes a visual editor that facilitates the creation of the documents that describe the games. The platform can be integrated with a Learning Management System. The engine uses the information from the Learning Management System (like the grade of a student) to adapt the game (Moreno-Ger et al., 2008b). In this work, the content is only adapted at the beginning of a session. Furthermore, the content in this system is mostly 2D, without any of the true elements of a 3D virtual world.

Celentano and Pittarello (2004) have developed another approach for adaptive navigation and interaction. So-called 'sensors' collect information about a user's behaviour and compare it with previous patterns of interaction to perform some activities of that pattern on behalf of the user. This approach focuses on the navigation and interaction, but not the emotions, of the learner. In the ELEKTRA project an adaptive framework for storytelling is developed. This project introduced a new terminology, namely macro and micro adaptivity. Macro adaptivity refers to traditional techniques of adaptation such as adaptive presentation and adaptive navigation, and are based on a fixed learner model (or adaptation model) and on typical (knowledge) assessments. Micro adaptivity affects only the presentation of a learning object or a learning situation.

In the 80Days project, being the follow-up project to ELEKTRA, the project team tried to assess the individual player's feelings, and emotional and affective responses, by looking at different criteria such as immersion, goals, autonomy, feedback, concentration and challenge. They assessed these criteria by using quantitative and qualitative methods such as survey questionnaire, interview, focus group, input observation, diary writing and psycho-physiological techniques. 80Days built on the results of the E-CIRCUS project and the VICTEC project which both focused on adapting synthetic characters (avatars) to promote social and emotional learning. Szita et al. (2006) developed a new approach called 'dynamic scripting' that is used to allow an avatar to adapt itself to the user's level. However, this adaptation was not considered in the context of any data about emotion. Gilleade and Dix (2004) considered frustration in the adaption of video games, but observed frustration only by monitoring button pressure on the gamepad.

Most adaptation in immersive virtual worlds has been focused on adaptive presentation, navigation and interaction for the individual learner and is based on typical (knowledge) assessments. Adaptation that considers emotions has started to appear in the field of educational games. However, this has not been examined in the context of Second Life where the system enables adaptation of the learning experience for the individual and for the group. Yet perhaps combining mixed reality, augmented reality or haptics may offer new and interesting developments in the field.

## Conclusion

This chapter has largely explored technological developments and suggested ways in which technology may be adapted and reused for Second Life. Many of these projects mentioned here do lack a strong pedagogical development component and most require further evaluation and long term research. Nevertheless such projects go some way to unpacking and addressing some of the technical difficulties which also occur in Second Life. The next chapter begins to explore ways of researching Second Life which may offer some purchase on how technological development can be used to improve learning and students' experiences of teaching.

# 10 Researching immersive virtual worlds

## Introduction

Considerable teaching development has taken place in Second Life and there is an increasing need to undertake sound research which can help improve practice. Many staff teaching in Second Life may evaluate their programmes but relatively few take on substantial research projects, and yet such studies are much needed. This chapter therefore offers some guidance in how to approach researching (in) Second Life. It begins by exploring methodologies that are useful for research in immersive virtual worlds. It draws on research approaches that have been adapted for research in Second Life and also presents new and emerging methodologies. Recent studies in this area are drawn on but the possibilities for the use of viral methodologies are also explored and ways are suggested in which research in immersive virtual worlds might be undertaken in the future.

## Research occurring in virtual worlds

To date there are a range of types, methodologies and methods of research being used in virtual worlds. The general tendency is to focus on inworld observation and interviews but there have also been countless surveys undertaken. The difficulty to date with much research in this area is that it focuses on methods and how to gather data, rather than locating the research in a methodological framework. Whilst this is understandable to some extent in a new field of research, it does tend to mean that considerable amounts of research are being undertaken in ways that lack rigour and plausibility because of the lack of a conceptual framework. The result is that there is little relationship between the methodology adopted and the way data are managed and interpreted. In this kind of research it is vital to have a conceptual framework, an exemplar of which is presented in Table 10.1.

**Table 10.1**   Developing a conceptual framework

**Research question**
**Methodology**
For example
↓

| Narrative inquiry | Virtual ethnography | Design methodology | Quantitative observational study | Action Research |
|---|---|---|---|---|

**Research design and relationship with methodology**
What will the research deal with?
How will you design the study to reflect the methodology?
↓

**Research methods**

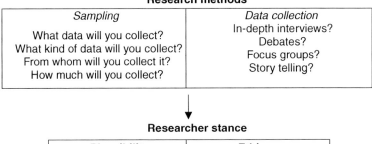

| *Sampling* | *Data collection* |
|---|---|
| What data will you collect?<br>What kind of data will you collect?<br>From whom will you collect it?<br>How much will you collect? | In-depth interviews?<br>Debates?<br>Focus groups?<br>Story telling? |

↓

**Researcher stance**

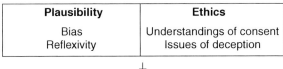

| **Plausibility** | **Ethics** |
|---|---|
| Bias<br>Reflexivity | Understandings of consent<br>Issues of deception |

↓

**Data management**

| Data analysis | Data interpretation |
|---|---|

↓

Presentation of findings
Conferences
Journal articles
Website
Blog
Book chapter

Yet there are many methodologies that have been developed for researching immersive virtual worlds as well as older ones that can be adapted (see for example Savin-Baden, 2010; Savin-Baden et al., 2010a; Savin-Baden and Tombs, 2010). When undertaking research in Second Life it is therefore important to consider a number of questions which will facilitate the development of a strong conceptual framework and a robust design for the research.

## Issues to consider

Many staff who begin researching in immersive virtual worlds are uneducated in qualitative research methods, and therefore often assume that 'interviewing' is qualitative research. If asked for a methodology they then refer to it as 'ethnography', yet it remains debatable as to whether interviews can in fact be classed as 'ethnographic'. However, it is important to consider the following issues when conducting research in Second Life:

### How will you decide on your research question?

The difficulty with designing a research question for exploring Second Life is that there is a tendency to try something either too large or too small. The questions that need to be asked are:

- What do you want to know?
- How will you find this out?
- What is manageable?
- How will you ensure your study is robust?

The easy option often seems to be to think of something you are interested in, rather than looking for gaps in the research or something that seems to be problematic. In contrast, by examining what has not been explored already or what is troublesome it will then be possible to develop a problem statement, and from that develop a research question. For example, I began by asking myself why people speak so little about space and how it is used in Second Life. This initial question prompted me to consider other issues such as identity, the constitution of avatars and the ways in which space is and is not used. The result was the following research question, and series of subsidiary questions: To what extent do avatars reflect and affirm the spatial metaphors and representations of space created in/by Second Life and what is the impact of this on how avatar identity is talked about and theorised?

1) How do avatars embody and occupy space?
2) What are the boundaries and violations of space in Second Life?

3) What cultural patterns and uses of space does Second Life encourage?

4) How do people see their avatar in the Second Life space?

Table 10.2 is useful for thinking through the development of your research question:

**Table 10.2**  Self-reflective questions for question development (from Major and Savin-Baden, 2010a: 47)

| | |
|---|---|
| *Question purpose* | Why am I developing the question in the first place? |
| | What knowledge is to be gained by conducting the synthesis? |
| | What problem can be solved? |
| | What do I hope to accomplish? |
| | Why do I want to accomplish this? |
| *Question source* | From where did the idea for the question germinate? |
| | What experiences led me to this question? |
| | What do I believe the answer to this question is? |
| *Question components* | Which variables are the most important to consider for the synthesis? |
| | What variables are the ones that are selected? |
| | What does the selection of these variables do to delimit the study? |
| | Why should this delimitation be done? |

## What kinds of research methodology will you adopt and why?

It is important to locate research in Second Life methodologically and consider whether you are using narrative inquiry, ethno-drama, co-operative inquiry or something else. Such a decision will inform your stance as a researcher, the way you conduct the study and the way data are collected, analysed and interpreted. Much of this will depend on your research question. For example, if you want to explore student experiences of Second Life, you could either use narrative inquiry to hear their stories or virtual ethnography to examine what they do in Second Life.

The research to date in immersive virtual worlds is complex and varied. Although there are many interesting studies and findings, there do seem to be methodological differences. For example, authors such as Hine (2000) have used virtual ethnography extensively, easily managed the sociological and methodological challenges of using ethnography in a new and complex space. Others have tended to shift real world practices into IVWs but largely shy away from the methodological difficulties this poses, but in ways that have enabled possibly more appropriate 'viral' methodologies to emerge (Carr and Oliver, 2009; Bayne, 2008). An example of this is Bayne's (2008) comparative analysis of the semiotics of a Virtual Learning Environment and a collaborative wiki. She looked in particular at the visual features and organisation of the two environments, and how they position participants and make ideological statements about education.

## The relationship between the methodology and the context of the research

As research in and into Second Life grows there has been a tendency to treat it as a different context from face-to-face research environments. Whilst there is difference, in terms of inworld observation and the complexities of consent, there is a tendency to overlay the context of research with possibly more complexity than is really necessary. I would suggest whether research is taking place in a hospital, school or diasporatic community there will always be contextual and ethical complexities. However, what is important is that contextual challenges are explored at the outset and dealt with in terms of the development of a robust methodology and research design. Some of the questions you may want to consider include:

- Am I researching Second Life or researching *in* Second Life?
- How does my methodology fit with Second Life as a context?
- What issues does this context raise for me as a researcher and in terms of the methodology I have chosen?
- What is my relationship with those from whom I collect data?
- How will the research context affect the way I collect data?
- What are the barriers I might encounter in a Second Life context?

## How will you analyse and interpret data?

The shift between analysis and interpretation is a complex one that is often overlooked. There is a tendency in Second Life research currently to undertake surveys and use descriptive statistics, which often give low response rates and sample sizes, meaning that the findings are rarely significant. It is probably better in terms of qualitative studies to opt for large scale data collection, trials or evaluation studies if you require your research to have a quantitative impact.

When interpreting qualitative data it is vital to keep participants at the centre of data interpretation. Data interpretation needs to be based predominantly in the experiences and perspectives of the participants we are seeking to represent and understand. For example, there is often a temptation to impose frameworks, categories or ideas on the data, instead of unravelling multiple meanings and engaging with the biographical and emotional meanings of data. It is therefore important to:

- Understand subtext. Subtext is about understanding the language participants are using in order to understand what is being said. Thus understanding the subtext requires that we help our participants to be reflexive and then that we tell their stories interpretatively as a snapshot of a moment in their lives.

- Negotiate and renegotiate meaning. For some researchers it seems acceptable to censor their own interpretations if participants do not agree with them. For other researchers, reaching some kind of agreement is seen as a vital part of the reflexive process. Yet the options about how interpretations are managed are complex and multifaceted so that decisions about power over, and ownership of, data (and interpretation thereof) tends to relate to the nature of the research topic and the type of data, as well as those involved.

- Recognise oppositional talk. Participants in research often share their perspectives in ways that are mechanisms for explaining and justifying their conduct and values. By exploring such perspectives it becomes possible to see how participants see and define themselves.

- Recognise organising principles. Organising principles are defined here as the categories used by people to justify, explain, defend and define themselves.

- Exploring metonymy and metaphor. The use of figurative terms and imagery is something that is also a useful means of interpreting data. Both metonymy and metaphor are often found in data, and unpacking what is meant by their use is a source of exploring the subtext.

Considering data in these ways will ensure that they are interpreted properly, rather than just presented descriptively in ways that do not do justice to the stories of those involved.

### What type of data will you collect?

In Second Life research a number of studies have been undertaken where the approach has been to 'just do some interviews', so that data collected are neither methodologically located nor thought through in terms of research design and style of interview. There are many approaches to collecting data and these need to reflect your methodology. For example, if using participatory action research rather than just using semi-structured interviews it is better to use interview debates with participants in their own setting, so that exploring ideas and sharing perspectives reflects the methodology undertaken.

### What are the ethical issues and how will you tackle them?

Ethical difficulties in Second Life seem to stem largely from issues of 'not knowing' that are not as prevalent as in face-to-face settings. There are concerns such as not knowing:

- who you are interviewing inworld
- if you are being watched
- if you are being filmed
- if people are lying because you cannot hear their inflections in text chat nor read their body language
- if people are joking or being ironic

Ethics in Second Life seems to cause considerable concern and yet in many ways the ethical issues in any research context are complex. Some of the areas that bear consideration include:

- Consent – what it is and who decides?
- Plausibility – this is a technique for ensuring rigour in that it involves locating the truths and the realities in the study, adopting a critical approach and acknowledging the complexities of managing 'truths' in research.
- Bias – how will you develop a better set of biases?
- To whom do the data belong?
- How do you know you are interviewing inworld (as opposed to face-to-face, or Skype) and if it matters or not?
- Agreements – be sure that everyone knows what they have signed up to and the consequences. Do not agree to anything you cannot ensure will happen such as sharing data and publishing together with fellow researchers.

### How will you ensure your data are plausible?

Plausibility (Major and Savin-Baden, 2010b) is the process of ensuring your research is rigorous and robust so that you can manage the research honestly. In the past qualitative research has used 'validity' but it is a term that has too much resonance with the quantitative paradigm and tends to ignore the complexities of qualitative research. However, issues connected with plausibility also collide with ethical concerns. For example, in their study on the dynamic relationship between chronic poverty, disability and occupation in households living on the margins of South African society, in peri-urban informal settlements and deep rural villages, Duncan and Watson (2010) state:

> We came to realise that socially responsible research ethics involves consciously adopting stances that would enable us to systematically think through why and how we participated in the world of those we engaged as informants. What counted as real in the relationships implicated by the research process depended,

in part, on where we positioned ourselves in relation to the politics of power.

(Duncan and Watson, 2010: 50)

Further, Macfarlane (2010: 20) also suggests that asking participants to sign a consent form is 'a defensive and quasi-legal means of trying to "protect" the university, and to some extent the researcher, from litigation or other accusations of wrong-doing'. Such issues and concerns may make us uncomfortable but they also introduce questions that need to be considered, and thus some further questions worthy of exploration might include:

- What strategies have I taken to ensure that I as a researcher am located within the research?
- How have I ensured that participant voices are portrayed honestly?
- How will I present, portray and represent multiple realities?
- How will I take into account people's stories in the arguments of the text?

## Methods, methodologies and design: what to use and why

The following section includes some suggestions of a number of methodologies which fit well when undertaking research in Second Life.

### Design-based methods

Design-based research is useful for Second Life as it combines both research and practice. Although this work did begin from a positivist standpoint (Brown, 1992; Collins, 1992), current work in this field predominantly argues for a synergy between research, design and action. Design-based research is defined by Wang and Hannafin as:

> a systematic but flexible methodology aimed to improve educational practices through iterative analysis, design, development, and implementation, based on collaboration among researchers and practitioners in real-world settings, and leading to contextually-sensitive design principles and theories.
>
> (Wang and Hannafin, 2005: 6–7)

Although there are a number of design-based approaches – and these are outlined by Wang and Hannafin, the approach that would seem to fit best with Second Life research is that developed by the Design-based Research Collective (2003). It adopts the following methods:

- conducted within a single setting over a long time
- uses iterative cycles of design, enactment, analysis and redesign
- acknowledges contextually dependent interventions
- seeks to document and connect outcomes with development process
- ensures collaboration between practitioners and researchers.
- results in the development of knowledge that can be used to inform practitioners and designers.

The reason this fits well with Second Life research is because it focuses on characteristics such as being pragmatic, interactive, flexible, integrative and contextual, so in many ways it has the feel of a viral methodology (which is discussed later in this chapter). Linked to this approach are developments in the use of design patterns research.

## Design patterns

This approach aims to make explicit a problem or pattern of difficulties that is recurrent and in the main relates to a given context. In practice patterns are located and organised into patterns languages. In the original work by Alexander (1979; Alexander et al., 1977), he argues that patterns can be seen as normative. Yet I would suggest this view is misplaced since people are always located in contexts which have at their heart issues of structure, power, agency and control, which will affect and change environments and patterns. However, the value of this approach to research in Second Life is in the move to the use of pedagogical design patterns. This can be seen in the JISC funded project Planet (Pattern Language Network for Web 2.0 in Learning) which used pattern language to explore the use of Web 2.0 technologies in their assessment, learning and teaching. In practice the project aimed to develop and demonstrate an effective community-based mechanism for capturing and sharing successful practice, based on the pattern approach. The authors (Finlay et al., 2009) developed the Participatory Pattern Workshop methodology which involves four stages:

1) sharing and exploring case stories from practice
2) eliciting and elaborating patterns across the case stories
3) mapping the relationship between patterns and learning design processes
4) applying patterns to new problem scenarios.

The idea is that the workshops are guided by facilitation activities and these are discussed in more depth in the link above. However, a more sociological perspective can be adopted by using virtual ethnography.

## Virtual ethnography

The work of Hine (2000) in this field has been seminal in terms of seeking to understand, from a sociological perspective, what people do on the Internet. Her stance has not been to focus on immersions as in more traditional ethnographic studies (for example Geertz, 1973), but instead to suggest it was important not to assume that by merely examining online actions and spaces it would be possible to understand what was or might be significant or meaningful. Thus virtual ethnography is seen as:

> ethnography *of, in* and *through* the virtual – we learn about the Internet by immersing ourselves in it and conducting our ethnography using it, as well as talking with people about it, watching them use it and seeing it manifest in other social settings.
>
> (Hine, 2000)

A number of authors have been using and exploring virtual ethnography and adopting different stances and theoretical perspectives. Table 10.3 provides three such examples:

**Table 10.3**  Examples of virtual ethnography

| Example | Use | Design | Theoretical framework | Challenges |
|---|---|---|---|---|
| Carr (2010) | Exploration of construction of online disability | Five semi-structured interviews | Cultural studies | Relationship between theoretical framework and data collection |
| Hemmi et al. (2009) | Pedagogical use of weblogs and wikis | Three degree programmes: divinity, design engineering and e-learning | Pedagogical exploration | Managing relationship between different types of data |
| Bardzell and Odom (2008) | Exploration of Gorean community in Second Life | Participant observation and in-depth interviews | Human–computer interaction | Interrelationship between methodologies adopted |

## Cognitive ethnography

This method is one of those that have stemmed from arguments such as that posed by Leander and McKim (2003), who have suggested the need to move beyond place-based ethnography. The central idea here then is in combining online and offline ethnographic methodologies. This approach explores the cognitive processes that affect the work carried out within a setting, whilst recognising in turn that the material world and social context of the actions carried out and the meanings attributed within the setting also affect the cognitive processes (Hollan et al., 2000). Hine (2007) argues that this approach is 'methodological response to e-science that builds on ethnographic traditions for understanding scientific practice.' Thus it seeks to combine science and meaning making within the same methodology. The work of Steinkuehler is an example of this approach. In a two-year online study, she used cognitive ethnography to describe 'specific cultures in terms of cognitive practices, their basis, and their consequences' in the context of Massively Multiplayer Online games (Steinkuehler 2007: 299). Her research design included:

1)   24 months of participant observation in the game
2)   several thousand lines of recorded transcribed observations of game play
3)   collections of game-related player communications (e.g. discussion board posts, chatroom and instant message conversations, emails)
4)   community documents (e.g. fan websites, community-authored game fictions, company- and community-written player manuals and guidebooks)
5)   unstructured and semi-structured interviews with multiple informants.

Further examples of research in this vein include Black and Steinkuehler (2009) who investigated the digital literacy practices of young people, and the virtual literacy ethnography of Teen Second Life, conducted by Gillen (2009).

## Future technology workshop

This is an approach developed by Vavoula and Sharples in which people with knowledge of the use of a particular area of technology:

> envision future activities related to technology design, build models of the contexts of use for future technologies, act out scenarios for use for their models, re-conceive their scenarios in relation to present-day technologies, list problems with implementing the scenarios, explore the gap between current and future technology and activity, and end by listing requirements for future technology.
>
> (Vavoula and Sharples, 2007: 393)

This approach must meet the following criteria:

a) minimal participant training
b) collaborative
c) direct input to design
d) cost-effective to run
e) relates people and technology
f) open-ended
g) pragmatic.

The advantage of this approach to Second Life is that it mirrors a participatory action research approach, but also fits with and informs other approaches such as human-centred systems design. In practice this can be used in Second Life by using research participants in the design both of the artefacts for learning and the learning itself.

## Futures and strategies for research in Second Life

The methodologies mentioned above are ones that have been in use for at least five years. The next section documents newer approaches that are useful for researching Second Life.

### Qualitative research synthesis

Qualitative research synthesis is an approach in which findings from existing qualitative studies are integrated using qualitative methods. It draws upon meta-ethnography as defined by Noblit and Hare (1988), but firmly locates the management and synthesis of findings in interpretivism. The purpose is to make sense of concepts, categories or themes that have recurred across a particular data set in order to develop a comprehensive picture of the findings. The approach requires adhering to a methodologically rigorous process while at the same time striving for transparency. Qualitative research synthesis, which relies upon sophisticated interpretivist methods for implementation, is one approach that has developed from these efforts. Synthesising existing information, through approaches such as qualitative meta-synthesis, provides a way to combine knowledge. Through qualitative meta-synthesis, large amounts of information are aggregated and then interpreted. The result is a report of research that presents a comprehensive view of knowledge contained in multiple studies. Qualitative research synthesis then allows researchers to summarise an existing body of knowledge and to make meaning of it. In this way, then, the information explosion around a given topic is in some ways contained, and knowledge becomes more comprehensible to others.

The difficulty with meta-analysis that is not located in an interpretive tradition is the propensity to decontextualise material, thin descriptions and ignore methodological difference.

### Stages of qualitative research synthesis

Qualitative research synthesis is undertaken at three levels described below:

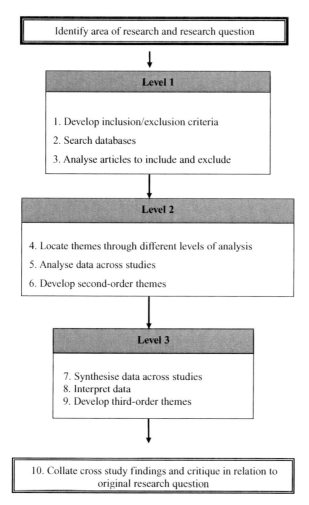

**Figure 10.1** Stages of qualitative research synthesis

For further details on how to undertake this, see Major and Savin-Baden (2010a).

The difficulty with qualitative research synthesis is that to date it is not clear how many studies could be located in order to undertake this approach for Second Life research. When using qualitative research synthesis it is clear that there is a poverty of methodological positioning, design and presentation of data in qualitative studies which means that many studies are likely to be excluded. However, it would seem that the need to synthesise qualitative studies has brought this to the fore and should result in an increase in the standard of published interpretive studies.

## Immersive ethnography

This is a methodology I have defined and is one which I suggest needs to be embraced and developed for Second Life, as it is one that combines ethnography with studies on immersion. In practice it is located at the boundaries of constructivism and constructionism, but takes a strongly interpretivist stance to data management. Immersive ethnography moves beyond virtual ethnography, suggesting that to gain in-depth understanding of Second Life researchers need to:

- live and work immersively in Second Life for over a year
- collect data through residing in Second Life and observing and participating in activities
- problematise culture norms
- see everything in Second Life as data.

Such immersion will result in the researcher feeling 'in' or 'part of' a virtual environment as they become absorbed or deeply involved. As mentioned earlier, immersion is a complex concept, thus for immersive research to take place it requires in-depth engagement with physical senses and mental processes within the environment, in order to understand the types of interaction, emotion, embodiment and technology involved. This approach therefore moves beyond just collecting interviews and watching what people do inworld. Rather the focus is on in-depth immersion whereby the researcher experiences a collision of being researcher, researched and participant.

## Viral methodologies

The notion of viral methodologies is that instead of methodologies being specifically 'located' in areas such as poststructuralism and constructivism, the underlying theories are seen as mutable and liquid. Although such methodologies are emergent and there is currently little written about them, they are based in the idea of viral learning (see for example, <u>Downes</u>). Such methodologies are interrupting theories and methods that change, are changed and are adapted according to researcher contexts, positionality and cultures. Such methodologies can be related to early work such as emergent design, where it is argued that the design is likely to change and shift through the course of the research. Thus the design emerges through a responsiveness to the participants and contexts (see for example, Lincoln and Guba, 1985). However, with viral methodologies it is the shifts, changes, ebbs and flows of the virality that makes these approaches different.

## Conclusion

Undertaking research in Second Life remains both challenging and exciting, and it affords the opportunity to develop new and emergent methodologies. However, with new methodologies and a changing landscape of immersive virtual worlds, it is vital that approaches are developed and used that are both rigorous and reflect the context of the research. The future of immersive virtual worlds also remains an interesting concern, and it is to this that we turn in the final chapter.

# 11 Futures and possibilities

Right now are we just inside a computer program?
*Your appearance now is what we call residual self image. It is the mental projection of your digital self*
This isn't real?
*What is real? How do you define real? If you were talking about what you can feel, what you can smell, and taste and see, then real is simply electrical signals interpreted by your brain*
(Wachowski and Wachowski, 2000)

## Introduction

Issues about what is real, what counts as simulations, and the role of immersion and emotion in learning, along with many other issues, continue to remain as debates across higher education. This final chapter begins by examining some of these issues and exploring some of the new technologies on the horizon that might inform future learning genres. It suggests that areas such as proxemics, haptics and mobile technologies bear further exploration and recommends that augmented and mixed reality can offer much to distance learning. However, the chapter also argues that Second Life is only the beginning of more profound technological and pedagogical shifts we are likely to experience in the future. In particular it offers new learning spaces that bring to the fore questions about social and formal learning and the extent to which learning in such threshold spaces bring new challenges to staff and students, in terms of the lexicon of capabilities they need for learning and teaching in higher education.

## Perspectives on the future

One of the pleasures and privileges of working in education research and in an area where new and innovative practices are being developed, is the opportunity to work across disciplinary boundaries. To help to develop the use of Second Life in sports science, speak with doctors in paediatric medicine and discuss options for its use in accounting education bring many challenges, not only about why we teach what we teach and how we teach it, but also decisions about what can be adopted across the boundaries and borders of our disciplines. This section suggests that a number of areas might usefully be explored both within and across diverse disciplines. Some of these suggestions are already being used comprehensively in some subjects, whilst others are being explored in just a few.

### Haptics and proxemics

Haptics is the use of technology that creates a sense of touch, such as vibration or movement, in order to enhance visual engagement in immersive virtual worlds. Gaining response feedback through gloves and using retinal projection in immersive virtual worlds is seen by some staff as important in improving the relationship between real-life and immersive virtual worlds so they become streamlined or even liminal in nature. Proxemics is the study of spatial distances between individuals in different cultures and situations, and was first defined by Hall who (1996) argued that humans have an innate distancing mechanism which helps regulate social situations. It is not clear what kinds of proxemics exist in Second Life, or the extent to which they really mirror real life as some such as Lowe (2003) suggest. Yet it would seem that identity and agency inworld is devolved in very novel ways, such as particular spaces, objects and activities causing avatars to respond in particular ways. This would seem to suggest an opportunity to challenge us to extend the simple author/avatar relationship to a broader consideration of agency, as it is reconstituted by the multiple relationships between author/avatar/world. This too raises questions about illusion and ownership, an area explored by Slater et al.

Slater et al. (2009) examined the idea of inducing illusory ownership of virtual limbs. They undertook three experiments that investigate how virtual limbs and bodies can come to feel like real limbs and bodies, and discussed related studies that indicate that the ownership illusion may be generated for an entire body. The findings of these studies suggest: 'that ownership of virtual limbs and bodies may engage the same perceptual, emotional, and motor processes that make us feel that we own our biological bodies' (p. 219). Slater has also suggested two concepts that might be useful for the exploration of the relationship between spaces and immersion on Second Life, although his work stems directly from virtual reality. Slater et al. (2009) argue for 'place illusion' and 'plausibility illusion' as concepts that are helpful in understanding why people respond in particular ways in virtual reality. 'Place illusion' (PI) is used for the type of presence that refers to the sense of 'being there' in spite of knowing that you are not, whereas 'plausibility illusion' (Psi) is defined as how the world is perceived: 'Psi is the illusion that what is apparently happening is really happening (even though you know for sure that it is not)' (p. 8).

What is interesting about this work is that Slater argues that both PI and immersion are motor functions, yet he also suggests that it is not possible to experience PI in desktop systems, giving the following example:

> A participant enters an immersive system such as tracked Cave or HMD system, and within that system approaches a (virtual) computer and starts to play a computer game or Second Life. Now how can we speak about PI in such a setup? They can sit by the (virtual) computer, pay attention to its display, and carry out valid actions with respect to the desktop system. But the 'host' environment, the one in which this is taking place is here also a virtual environment. So where is PI in all this? Just as immersion is bound to a particular set of valid actions that support perception and effectual action within a particular virtual reality so it is reasonable to consider that the same is the case with respect to PI.
>
> (Slater et al., 2009: 6)

What Slater largely seems to be suggesting is that immersion is related to 'qualia', the illusion of being there. Immersion depends predominantly on the level of qualia, which is seen to be higher in virtual reality than in desktop systems such as Second Life which require more deliberate attention. Yet the sense of immersion does seem to be affected by emotion that may emerge directly from immersion or illusion. For example, there have been various studies of the visual cliff scenario (Gibson and Walk, 1960) where the participant is in an unusual room where the floor is just a narrow ledge around an open hole that exposes another room 6 metres below. Most of the participants edge their way carefully around the ledge at the side rather than simply gliding across the non-existent (virtual) pit. Similar concerns about drowning and getting stuck in buildings have also been reported in studies on Second Life – although these were not undertaken directly into the area of immersion (for example, Savin-Baden, 2010). Thus it would seem for Slater's work that there are levels of immersion and that PI is likely to be different in different environments.

## Spatial interaction

An innovative model of spatial interaction was developed by Benford and colleagues in 1993 (Benford and Fahlén, 1993; Benford et al., 1994) for use in virtual environments. Following this initial model a number of other studies built on this but as yet it is not a model that has been adapted for Second Life. The authors argue that it is a model that provides flexible support for managing conversation between groups, and can be used to control interactions among other kinds of objects as well. The model centres on the concepts of aura, nimbus, focus and adapters. Aura is the area around and which bounds an object or person, adapters are objects that modify aura, focus or nimbus, such as the process of picking up an object. Focus is awareness of an object and nimbus is a subspace that affects and influences objects: They explain:

> As with aura, awareness levels are medium specific. Awareness between objects in a given medium is manipulated via *focus* and *nimbus*, further subspaces within which an object chooses to direct either its presence or its attention. More specifically, if you are an object in space: The more an object is within your focus, the more aware you are of it. The more an object is within your nimbus, the more aware it is of you.

Thus they suggest

> *The level of awareness that object A has of object B in medium M is some function of A's focus in M and B's nimbus in M.* [italics in original]
>
> (Benford et al., 1994: 226)

In their model Benford and Fahlén (1993) suggest three ways of manipulating aura, focus and nimbus:

1)  Through movement and orientation
2)  By changing parameters such as focal length
3)  Through using adapter objects which will modify aura, focus or nimbus.

In practice this model is useful because it could help those using Second Life for teaching to measure distance and orientation, but perhaps more importantly it offers a means of conversation management and dynamic interaction, whereby an object (such as a tool) reacts when it is approached by an avatar. Although some of this kind of work is being developed in Second Life, what Benford et al. have delineated, examined and developed is an understanding of the dimensions of a virtual space. The notion of space and spatial focus in Second Life remains relatively under explored and it is difficult for staff to help students filter information, gain their attention or deal with over talking and overhearing. Finding ways of adapting this model would be useful for dealing with some of these issues.

## Hybrid spaces

Benford (2009) explores the relationship between real and virtual spaces, revisiting some previous work carried out, in order to examine the relationship between the structure of hybrid physical-digital spaces from the fields of ubiquitous computing, virtual reality and mixed reality. What is particularly interesting is the relationships he explores between these spaces, in particular the concepts of overlay and agency. He presents Milgram and Kishino's mixed reality continuum (1994):

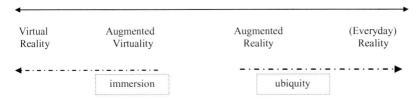

**Figure 11.1** Mixed reality continuum (Milgram and Kishino, 1994)

At one end of this continuum lies everyday physical reality and at the other is an immersed virtual reality in which the participant is completely immersed in a computer generated virtual world. The areas in between vary from spaces where the participant primarily inhabits the physical but is working in the virtual – a managed learning environment could be located here; to augmented reality where the participant inhabits an online virtual world, but which is made live with information from the physical world; this could be the use of Second Life with live feeds into problem-based scenarios, such as breaking news or weather reports. What we are seeing here is the relationship between adjacency and overlay. In Second Life the use of feeds and real life data being streamed in uses overlay, so that this results in augmented virtuality.

However, adjacency emerges from the idea of the concept of a mixed reality boundary which is where there is a two way portal between the physical and virtual worlds. Thus:

> Participants in a physical space see a persistent projected view of a virtual space on the wall while participants in the virtual world see a persistent live video texture looking back into the physical world. The two are then aligned in such a way (and enhanced with an additional audio channel) to create the effect of a two way window so that each kind of participant can look from their space into the other. Multiple mixed reality boundaries can then be used to connect many physical and virtual spaces into a more complex hybrid structure, in much the same way that physical spaces are connected in a building.
>
> (Benford, 2009: 3)

In practice this means that in a physical office it is possible to make it appear to be adjacent to a virtual office; it is as if the virtual office is an extension beyond the screen: they are not overlaid, they are next to each other. What is important for future developments of this work in

Second Life is that it offers a language and structure to begin to make sense not only of the developments occurring in Second Life, but also a means of examining the diversity of studies and activities taking place in other fields that can be used and built on for Second Life teaching in higher education.

## Gesture-based media and Motion Capture

Gesture in real life is an important part of conversation and certainly in Second Life it would improve communication and dialogic learning in particular. One of the frustrations staff and students experience in Second Life is the inability to use gestures effectively. For some it is an area that is ignored and worked around, for others it is seen as problematic. Yet the ability to use gestures would be helpful to enable learners to engage in virtual activities in ways that mirror real life. What is important here is that gestures allow communication and the manipulation of content to be undertaken intrusively. This would mean learners would not have to consider how to move an object or think about how to point or smile using an emoticon, but would just do it. Gesture-based tools and interfaces would then begin to change Second Life interaction so it became increasingly intuitive. This kind of activity could be developed further by the use of Motion Capture. This involves the use of sensors on clothing in order to link real-world movement with inworld movement for activities such as inworld performance and theatre. These kinds of activities and interfaces would then begin to shift Second Life into a more augmented reality environment.

## Mixed Reality and Augmented Reality

The basic idea is that through different media there is a merging of real life and immersive virtual worlds so that there is little transition between the two, in similar ways that are used by current Wii technology. Mixed Reality is seen as a method for integrating virtual and physical spaces much more closely, and attempts to connect people who are physically remote from each other within the same space. It is defined by the relationships that are imposed between the physical and virtual, as demonstrated in Figure 11.1 above. Augmented Reality tends to place more emphasis on the physical, so that information from virtual space is accessed from within physical space. An example of this would be the projection of Second Life into a physical space such as a real life conference, whereas augmented virtuality augments virtual space with aspects from physical space, so there is a greater sense of overlay, as discussed above. However, although this can be a helpful distinction, the increasing blurring of boundaries between these types of reality is mounting, and it would seem that we will soon reach a point when adjacency and overlay collide.

## Mobile technologies

Mobile learning centres on the idea that it is the learner who is mobile rather than necessarily the technology. According to Sharples et al. (2005), mobile learning is based on the assumption that considerable learning takes place not only outside the classroom, but also that people create sites for learning within their surroundings:

> We suggest that the implications of this re-conception of educa-tion are profound. It describes a cybernetic process of learning through continual exploration of the world and negotiation of meaning, mediated by technology. This can be seen as a chal-lenge to formal schooling, to the autonomy of the classroom and to the curriculum as the means to impart the knowledge and skills needed for adulthood. Nevertheless, it can also be an opportunity to bridge the gulf between formal and experiential learning, open-ing new possibilities for personal fulfilment and lifelong learning.
> (Sharples et al., 2005)

Before long it will be possible to have effective graphics and interface so that it will be possible to use Second Life on a mobile phone (not just by us-ing interfaces such as Sparkle). Yet the idea that the mobility is connected to the learner rather the technology introduces interesting issues about the notion of learning contexts. Ramsden (1984; 1992) suggested that a stu-dent's perception of the learning context is an integral component of his learning. The learning context is created through students' experience of the constituents of the programmes on which they are studying, namely teaching methods, assessment mechanisms and the overall design of the curriculum. Therefore students, Ramsden suggests, respond to the situa-tion they perceive, which may differ from that which has been defined by educators. Yet often, however much it is denied, educators tend to think of learning contexts as static environments. What this brings into question is how these new learning contexts can be used, enhanced and managed by staff – since it would seem with such mobility that both the context and the control will increasingly reside with the learners, something we should perhaps take on sooner rather than later. Perhaps we should be us-ing Wikitude World Browser across all our programmes so that students can view, access and customise their learning on the move.

# Photorealism

A further area of development and one that also seems to spark contro-versy is that of the use of photorealism in Second Life. Although the origi-nal term refers to the genre of painting based on a photograph, it is referred to in Second Life as the highly realistic reproduction of objects and build-ings from real life. In short the idea is that the artist uses the camera to gain information and then uses mechanical or semi-mechanical means to transfer the information to the canvas, with the result that the finished work appears photographic. In virtual worlds photorealism has been used in augmented reality to create realistic environments which includes the use of bumps and shadowing, the idea being that the image produces the same visual response as the scene. However, because of the limitation in Second Life in terms of 'prim' restrictions and, for many academics, the ability to script, very high levels of photorealism are not possible. To combat this, many photographers in Second Life also use Photoshop to enhance their images and many people are creating graphics on other programmes and then importing them into Second Life. However, authors such as Durand (2002) contend that virtual worlds often have to be more *convincing* rather than *realistic*. The real shift is likely to come when it is possible to use one's real-life face, with motion capture, on one's avatar. There are many people who want to present their real life self in Second Life and therefore currently make their avatar look as much like them as possible, but there are other platforms that are even more realistic. For example, the realXtend avatar can use Facegen's photofit feature to make quite accurate faces and it would seem that Ludocraft may soon bring face tracking and facial animation to realXtend.

Whatever the new and emerging developments that are occurring and can be adopted and adapted for Second Life, it is important not to lose the sense that learning in spaces such as Second Life brings with it not only the possibilities for creativity and innovation, but also the sense of being and living and learning on a threshold, and locating learning in threshold spaces.

# Second Life as a threshold space

The idea of a threshold space is that there are times in learning and teach-ing when there is a feeling of being on the edge of learning something, or engaging with something quite new and different. This could be an encounter with a threshold concept, but more often in relation to Second Life it is the realisation – possibly an epiphany, where a new way of see-ing or doing something occurs. In the threshold space there is a sense of being on the brink, but often in a comfortable stuck place, as there is a sense of flow, an idea that this emerging idea will work. In the main, staff and students often feel worried rather than excited about being stuck; it invariably begins with a negative experience, normally painful to wrestle with, and can be worsened by avoidance or retreat, although ultimately it can be positive if dealt with successfully. Most movements into threshold space are often positive and result in new insights. For example, there is a sense that Second Life has not only generated its own culture, but that it has also enabled the creation of threshold spaces for the development of social and emotional capital. Some of this seems to be because the culture is one of residence; people live, work, teach and make homes in this culture, they do not just use it like a virtual learning environment. Emotional capital emerges because of the way in which spaces and identities are imbued with a sense of ownership and embodiment, which is not seen in the same way in other environments such as Blackboard. The sense of 'feeling' hurt or upset if someone knocks down your building are very strong, and introduces questions about what embodiment, presence and immersion mean in these spaces. Yet at the same time Second Life also introduces other interruptions about what it means to be a teacher in Second Life. Our very pedagogical stances and identities shift, change and move, and this brings into question the extent to which it is possible to transfer our authority as teachers from one world to another. Yet there remain other issues barely addressed in this text, such as the value of co-presence for learning. There is often an assumption that the technical and the social are different spheres and increasingly there is a view that the technical can be attributed with faster ways of learning and changed cultural practices. Yet Second Life seems to have created a specialist discourse community invoking particular genres and a specific lexus as well as being strongly participatory in nature (see for example, Nystrand, 1982; Porter, 1992; Swales, 1990). Mercer suggests:

> A discourse community is a community in which people do not necessarily live together or ever see each other face-to-face, but where language (either spoken, written or digital) is used among themselves to pursue some common goals
>
> (Mercer, 1996: 84)

It could be suggested that if co-presence is not seen as valuable by staff then those staff should not use Second Life – but this would seem rather stark. Perhaps Putnam's perspective is more helpful:

> For most of us, our deepest sense of belonging is to our most intimate social networks, especially family and friends. Beyond

that perimeter lie work, church, neighbourhood, civic life, and [an] assortment of other 'weak ties'.

(Putnam, 2000: 274)

## The end and the beginning: living and working at the interstices

As we come to the close of this text Second Life continues to develop and change. There are promises of updates, changes and flexibility. Clearly using Second Life has changed staff perspectives of what is possible in a whole host of ways. Distance education seems more embodied, immersion is expected to enhance learning. Play and experimentation – despite the increasingly performative culture, seems to have made a return. Although there are still many difficulties with Second Life in terms of acceptability, access and perceived relative value, it is neither a technology nor a learning space that is likely to disappear. Whilst for many staff in higher education there is still a degree of cynicism about its value, the impact of it is possibly greater than we currently imagine. This is because the use and implantation of Second Life and immersive worlds in general have helped staff reconsider learning, challenged them to take a new view about the purpose of higher education, and enabled them to question the value of current higher education provision.

As we reach the second decade of the millennium, the future and promised cuts in higher education mean that university management are already planning strategies to keep their universities in existence. The focus is not only on staff reduction and increasing student numbers, but on improving the student experience. Although the latter is largely to ensure fees and retentions, resourceful academics will see this not as an obstacle but as an opportunity. Student experience can be enhanced through Second Life, particularly for those on distance programmes, but the value of Second Life across the disciplines I suspect has yet to be realised. Second Life is a learning space, a threshold space that brings to the fore new and interesting questions about what it is that learning should be. Many students today play computer games and use a Wii as well as learn on the move through mobile technology. Social networking, from Facebook to Twitter, changes and develops daily. Nevertheless there are staff that still remain convinced that social networking, games and multitasking should be kept out of learning institutions – which would seem not only naive but misplaced. For example, I was recently at a dinner with two university managers who were discussing whether students really did concentrate when listening to music, chatting on Facebook and writing a considered essay. I suggested that this was the norm as far as I was concerned – and that I would expect students to twitter and email during lectures. They were shocked and appalled. The important thing now is to harness rather than ignore these technologies. I doubt students will stop texting and twittering – and I certainly think we should use it rather than ignore it. To allow students social networking in higher education openly is surely better than giggling and covert texting occurring at the back of the lecture hall.

Yet this is only the beginning – haptics, gesture-based interfaces and motion capture are all on the way. The recent mock up of Milo, an artificial intelligence character that can interact with you through Natal which is an Xbox 360 motion control system, referred to as a 'controller-free gaming and entertainment experience,' has courted controversy. Although this is generally referred to as a game in which the player interacts with a young child by performing real-life actions, the implication has been that an avatar could be trained to be responsive – and it does seem to be something that is likely to be built in the near future. Certainly it would seem that we are on the cusp of some large technological shifts, and not engaging with these will merely show the cracks in our idealism and the fractures in our pedagogies.

## Conclusions

Second Life and related technologies may not be comfortable spaces and places for academics, but that would seem to be a good thing. Discomfort, disjunction, aporia, stuck places; whatever versions of these that are encountered need to be seen as a possibility, a new learning space, even as a privileged place from which to move off into something different and strange. Perhaps my stance is naive and utopian. Writing this book has been a stretching challenge, but one that has given me the opportunity to consider a range of issues and literature. What strikes me most of all is that whatever we have use of that can be adapted or adopted for higher education should be harnessed to improve student learning. For some, possibly many, Second Life is now a norm, for others it is something to ignore or abandon at all costs. Yet higher education is on the move, and technology is something we need to take with us into this unknown future, whilst recognising that living at the interstices of learning and technology are important places to stand.

# Appendix A
# Second Life: module exemplar

## 1. Module summary

### Aims and summary

Second Life is a multi-user virtual environment (think World Wide Web but in 3D). Individuals create their own virtual alter-egos and create, build, dance, buy, sell and get up to practically anything that is humanly possible (and several things that are not) in this alternate world.

Essentially a game, albeit one with limited rules and no specific goals, Second Life is a world where students can interact in real time with a global community, try out ideas and explore real world possibilities in relative safety. Projects that in the real world would cost thousands can be explored in this virtual world for free or very minimal outlay, with the possibility of then taking new understanding and learning back into the real world.

The aim of this module is to introduce students to this environment; teach them how to use the various functions within the 'game', building, scripting etc., to work on specific inworld tasks; and finally in small groups to formulate a project proposal and carry out a specific task. This could be anything from running a small business, designing clothes or building a racing car to making a short film.

### Module size and credits

| | |
|---|---|
| *Module size* | Half |
| *CATS points* | 10 |
| *ECTS credits* | 5 |
| *Open/restricted* | Open |
| *Availability on/off campus* | On/Off |
| *Total student study hours* | 100 |
| *Number of weeks* | 10 |
| *School responsible* | ART AND DESIGN |
| *Academic year* | 2007–8 |

### Entry requirements (pre-requisites and co-requisites)

None.

### Composition of module mark (including weighting of components)

100% coursework.

### Pass requirements

40%.

### Courses for which this module is mandatory

None.

### Courses for which this module is a core option

None.

## 2. Teaching, learning and assessment

### Intended module learning outcomes

The intended learning outcomes are that on completion of this module you should be able to:

- Understand the key functions and tools of Second Life and be able to use them effectively.
- Design a creative response to a set brief, including project management planning, analysis of market potential (where relevant) and resource needs.
- Have some understanding of the complexities, problems and possible benefits of working creatively, collaboratively, online.
- Reflect upon your employability competencies and career management skills and plan for your future development.

### Indicative content

- Exploration of the functions, tools, and environment within Second Life.
- Creating a project brief.
- Negotiating and running a project.
- Team work/problem solving.

Whilst completing this module you will also undertake activities online, within the Employability Learning Programme (ELP). ELP is designed to help you develop your career management skills and learn more about employers' requirements of graduates. The ELP will inform your future development of employability competencies using personal development planning and will be assessed by means of an e-portfolio.

### Teaching and learning methods

The sessions (two hours per week) will take place in a computer lab and initially will need all students to be present in person. Activities will include building, scripting, texturing, and an exploration of the wider community that exists within Second Life. Once students are more confident it will be possible to run the course entirely online. Students will need to attend the designated sessions, whether in person or online, but will be expected to arrange their own times to meet up in order to carry out the project.

### Composition of module mark

### Method of assessment

- Method of Assessment: Planning and realisation of project and a final mark moderated after group presentation (Pass/Fail), and e-portfolio assessed as Pass/Fail.
- Reassessment Mode: Planning and realisation of project and a final mark moderated after group presentation (Pass/Fail), and e-portfolio assessed as Pass/Fail.
- Method of Reassessment: Submission of required work by set deadline. Failed e-portfolios to be reassessed.

### Special features

N/A

### Date of last amendment

20/2/2007

## 3. Module resources

### Essential reading

www.secondlife.com tutorials, wikis, forums

### Recommended reading

Second Life the official guide 793.9325369 SEC
YouTube: secondlife films and tutorials
http://home.ched.coventry.ac.uk/caw/harvard/index.htm

### Required equipment

Computer and Internet access (this could be entirely on site).

# Appendix B
# Dealing with challenges and mistakes in Second Life

Many of the difficulties related to the use of Second Life occur because of either complete unfamiliarity with immersive virtual worlds or a familiarity with gaming that tends to get in the way of seeing the educational value of this type of immersive world.

Some of the challenges at the outset include:

- Deciding initially whether or not to adopt Second Life (or another immersive world)
- Deciding initially how relevant it is to a particular discipline and institution
- If the decision is taken to buy an island, deciding how staff might be encouraged to use it.

It is important to ensure that the development and use of Second Life for both staff and the institution is not only a pedagogical design process but also a community building experience. However, some of the concerns raised by staff are outlined below.

## Concerns

### Second Life doesn't fit well with many current teaching practices

In the same way that past adoption of new innovations such as PBL or CAD did not fit well with established teaching practices, and ultimately required curricular redesign, SL often does not fit well with many current teaching practices. Currently, modules and programmes are designed with a focus on real life teaching practices, and in particular the way the discipline affects that and the way knowledge is viewed. There needs to be, then, more exploration of the relationship between the learning activities, the medium and the way knowledge is to be managed. To focus on *how* and *where* students learn before considering what content is to be covered will help to shift the focus. However, with the current tendency to over-structure higher education systems and practices, managing such a shift remains difficult and problematic.

## It is seen as too quirky and too clunky

Staff often ask what the purpose of using Second Life is – many just see its use as something quirky. However, a study by Conradi et al. (2009) established that staff found high levels of student engagement in the use of Second Life problem-based learning and considered the scenarios to be fit for purpose and usable within the course. Staff nevertheless suggested that there was a need for more intrinsic feedback and for students to be able to access background learning material. Anecdotal complaints from other staff across the higher education sector tend to focus on Second Life running slowly, the graphics being poor and taking a long time to render. Yet the graphics continue to improve and there are increasing solutions (such as PIVOTE), discussed in more depth in Chapter 9, which are reducing the problems of slowness and perceived 'clunkiness'.

It is also difficult to find other people at ease in Second Life if you do not know their avatar name, and this can prove frustrating. On the other hand, there are many other staff who would equally argue that dealing with these issues is just part of the process and peculiarity of working and learning in Second Life. There have been many times over the past few years when Second Life has not worked effectively because of constant updates, but in the main it is more stable now. The new version released in 2010 has also overcome many of the earlier difficulties as well as providing much improved graphics. However, no technology is ever entirely reliable and those who have been using Second Life for some time appear to have become used to the ebbs, flows and inconsistencies – and in the end just see it as part of working with that medium.

## Relatively little research that indicates what works best and what does not

Interest in the area and studies into what is occurring continue to flourish, but much of the discussion about what works and what does not is largely passed on via the various Second Life discussion forums. The reviews of research undertaken to date (see for example, Savin-Baden et al., 2010b) seem to indicate rather broadly that Second Life is:

- Being used for scenarios, simulations and role-plays where the semiotic resources offer a pedagogic context not available else-where. This is particularly apparent in the take-up of IVWs for problem-based learning and related approaches, in which complex decisions must be taken in real time by professional teams required to apply theory to practice in complex and high-pressure situations.

- Used for the development of capabilities for teamwork or team building, particularly in distance contexts where participants cannot easily form these relationships via discussion forums.
- Adopted as an environment that has particularly helpful uses that can be harnessed for teaching such as in computing, design and architecture.

## Common mistakes

Many of the mistakes in Second Life tend to occur because of familiarity with the environment or because of misplaced pedagogical assumptions about using the medium for teaching and learning:

### Complaining

One of the most common mistakes about using Second Life is to complain. It is an interesting technology and can be used to enhance learning, but it does take a bit of getting used to – and for the most part, complaining does not help. Some of the most common complaints include:

1) High bandwidth and good graphics cards prevent global use of such platforms for learning
2) Lack of safety – the open nature of SL means it cannot be used in schools, some universities currently disallow it and it is costly to put behind the university firewall
3) Much of the current use of Second Life in higher education is pedagogically ill-informed and the reasons for its use based more around interest in technology than pedagogy
4) Although SL was not designed for learning it is being used for learning, and there are many features available in it taking up 'space' that could be stripped down for more effective learning use
5) The extra features not required for learning add to the waiting time required for SL to render on screen
6) The graphics, for some people, are seen as basic compared with computer games and so are sometimes seen as a barrier. This could of course be overcome by improving the graphics, but higher education would not necessarily see this as a worthy cost.

Many of these difficulties can and are being resolved, so there is sense in learning to use it by being patient and trying out different things.

## Not setting up the learning session and environment properly

One of the most common mistakes staff make is just to give students the co-ordinates of where to meet in SL and expect them to turn up there. There do need to be initial preparations such as:

- Setting up a Second Life group for your students
- Sign-posting and labelling an environment clearly
- Making sure that it is a lively session with group activities rather than a passive exercise like reading text, which of course could be done on other platforms.

## Forgetting to check when upgrades will occur

The Second Life community and wiki provide information about when upgrades will occur, so it is important to check the site regularly so that you can, if necessary, move teaching sessions in advance. It can be demoralising for students who have put aside time to attend a Second Life session when a mandatory upgrade occurs instead, and they do not find this out until just before the start of the session. Fortunately this has become less regular and in general now only occurs once every 3–4 months.

## Poor and ineffective use of the space

There is a tendency to impose real life teaching on Second Life, instead of thinking differently about what learning might mean in this space. Sometimes this means using activities that might not be seen as learning, such as building and yet this can be a helpful ice-breaker. At the same time there can be a tendency to over structure, such as:

- Making orientation sessions too structured (squeezing the fun out of the platform). It is important to remember that a lot of Second Life has to be learned by experimentation, and not by learning a list of functions.
- Forgetting that Second Life is very new and that there is no 'proper' way to engage with it, it is an emergent culture.

## That you can be a member of lots of Second Life groups

In 2009 you could still only be a member of twenty-five Second Life groups and this means that networking and communication can be difficult. Fiona Littleton at the University of Edinburgh suggests that Linden Lab has still not really seen the value of social networking in Second Life. In fact I would suggest that in many ways Second Life rather stands against the current trends in the social networking arena, where the focus is on links, friendships, shared networks and community building, which the design of Second Life seems to disable rather than enhance.

### Failing to provide students with basic guidance that will help them into the space more easily

Whilst some of these suggestions may sound obvious it is surprising how often staff fail to:

- Teach students how to sit down!
- Show students how to use the mini-map
- Schedule a 'warm-up' and 'cool-down' time for students to chit-chat and socialise before and after sessions. Doing this will help them to negotiate the social challenges of Second Life.

### Failing to help students to develop beyond the basics

It is easy to assume that once students can move and communicate that this is enough for a seminar, when in fact it is useful to:

- Be clear about the difference between IM, chat and voice chat and how they can be used
- Encourage experimentation and play.

### Things change you don't expect

The Coventry University Island is open to all visitors; however during testing sessions with open permissions on the holodeck, participating students sometimes accidentally changed the scenario during strategy management. Due to this, limited permissions have been put onto the holodeck so that only staff can start up the scenarios.

### Interaction is easier in Second Life than discussion forums

While some staff feel that engagement, communication and community building is easier in Second Life, others do not. This may of course re-late to the fact that it is synchronous rather than asynchronous. Hamish Macleod, University of Edinburgh feels that he has to work harder in Second Life than discussion forums, because in Second Life people can 'see' when he is not saying or doing anything. The idea of 'being' embodied in Second Life would seem to result in some staff feeling pressurised to speak and engage in ways they may not do in discussion forums.

# Common assumptions

When discussing assumptions, the general view is that staff and students either love or hate Second Life and manage their assumptions accordingly. Yet this seems not to be the case – although there inevitably remain the flag-waving evangelists and the hard-nosed cynics. The following issues have emerged from discussion with staff and have come from their experiences as both teachers and learners in Second Life.

## Second Life is so complex to use that it is not worth the trouble

The tasks of downloading Second Life, getting an avatar and learning to travel does demand a little time and persistence to begin with, and this is often the most difficult part of getting started with Second Life. It will obviously be more difficult if your university refuses to allow its use but that is related to internal politics, and not the media itself. However, in terms of the initial difficulties of using Second Life there are a number of ways around these, such as developing your own orientation areas that staff and students can enter using teleporting. It is also possible to develop induction sessions and private spaces such as those suggested by Truelove and Hibbert (2008).

## It is a game and teaching should be developed to mirror games

The issue of whether Second Life is a game (MMORG) remains debatable. In spite of that, one of the difficulties for some staff is that gamers and some learning technologists assume that Second Life will somehow be better if teaching within it was designed more like a game. Ramondt (2008) for example offers some sound arguments to this effect and provides a helpful comparison of Second Life and World of Warcraft. Nonetheless, to overlay learning in Second Life with the perspective that it will necessarily be better if it is designed as a game somewhat misses the pedagogical point. The challenge and usefulness of a 3D virtual world lies in the fact that it can be both a game and not a game – that its very flexibility and (relative) lack of rules renders it useful to a wide range of purposes in higher education, which would be lost if the focus was solely on game design.

## Students will not adapt to it

This may be the case, but it is interesting to note that it takes very little time (about a minute) for students to speak of themselves in Second Life as 'me' rather than 'my avatar'. There is a sense then that students quite readily relate to their inworld position, and begin to operate as an extension or representation of their identity inworld more quickly than is initially expected by staff.

### It is a very dangerous place and is full of pornography

Although there have been instances reported of abuse and pornography (and certainly the world media takes great interest in broadcasting all the unpleasant things about Second Life) those using it in higher education have largely been able to avoid these areas. Additionally the introduction of Zindra, the adult grid, in June 2009 seems to have relieved some of these difficulties. For those new to Second Life some suggestions are:

- Avoid buildings with no windows
- When you take free buildings from the freebie dungeon check what is inside them before you place them on your university island
- Avoid places where large numbers of people are congregating as they are likely to be involved in cybersex
- Try to avoid wearing scanty clothing such as thongs, leather and sporting whips, it might give the wrong impression
- Ensure you set your institution's island settings to prevent the use of adult content
- If you are really worried lock down your island so others may not enter
- If you are not just worried but veering towards paranoia, you could label buildings such as theatres that might look like night clubs, but this does seem rather extreme.

I have spent hundreds of hours inworld, but have only experienced one incident, where I was hit violently over the head by a sinister cloaked and masked figure, who then ran off. While these incidents are often regaled with amusement at conferences, they have probably occurred relatively infrequently.

### Students will not be upset by griefing because it is not real

Griefing is carried out by griefers, individuals who seem to enjoy causing others grief, such as bumping or hitting them and generally being unpleasant, especially to newbies. They may be found at Infohubs, Welcome Areas or Help Island Public; some staff advise not sending students to Help Island Public at all because of the level of griefing. In 2009–10 there has been an increase in griefing in Second Life and in general it is something that does worry and even scare students. Discussion with them and explaining ways to manage griefing is important to carry out early on in the course.

### Collaboration is necessarily a part of learning and that it is easy to set up

The fact that individuals are represented by avatars in Second Life does not automatically aid collaborative work. Things to consider:

- That being 'embodied' by an avatar can lead to a heightened sense of being co-present with other individuals online – but not everyone experiences this
- The lack of non-verbal cues and the delays in communication caused by text or voice chat mean that Second Life struggles to support the kind of interpersonal cues and immediacy needed for close collaboration.

### Second Life and real life teaching is really quite similar

A further common assumption is that it is easy, straightforward and possible to transpose real life teaching into Second Life, but to do so would be to mistake the educational purposes of this kind of learning. Thus building lecture theatres and presenting PowerPoint inworld is possible and for distance students this can be useful.

### Voice communication via a microphone will be more effective than text chat

In fact the lack of non-verbal cues and believable lip-sync (although this has improved considerably) within Second Life causes voice chat to present a seeming sense of the disembodiment of avatars. This then generates a feeling that you are involved in a phone conference whilst looking at a collection of mannequins on screen. Staff experienced in Second Life tend to argue:

- The use of Second Life can seem nullified when voice is used, unless students are attempting a focused task in which their avatars become simply tools to achieve a goal rather than an immersed embodiment of their persona
- The problem of the slight delays which the system suffers from, and using voice chat can cause exhaustion and confusion, similar to that of a traditional phone conference.

Text chat has its own failings as it can be slow and fractured, but it is worth remembering that multiple people can type at the same time whereas only one can talk. An experienced group can communicate surprisingly efficiently using text chat, a communication paradigm that is becoming ever more part of our culture.

### Social pressures within Second Life will always be a problem

Second Life is a social space and all students will feel a need to distinguish themselves from others and often to demonstrate their level of expertise relative to the environment they are in. This immediately leads to a preoccupation with hairstyles, clothing and general appearance. Ways around this include:

- Recognising that not looking like a default avatar or a 'n00b' is very important to many, so it is worth planning in time for students to play with their appearance before attempting any specific teaching.
- Using appearance play as an ice-breaker which can also help students learn some key basic skills (camera control, navigation, communication).

### What you look like in Second Life is not that relevant to teaching (uniform, crazy hair etc.)

It is a mistake to imagine that it is possible to use Second Life without aspects of social and identity issues coming into play. Avatars encourage a persuasive from of anthropomorphism leading even a small group of students on a private island to start to generate a 'society' which is concerned with more than just the learning in hand. If you are wary of this aspect of Second Life then it will be more fruitful to use a different platform, rather than to try and 'lock down' these effects of the virtual world.

### 'Gamers' will like Second Life or understand how to use it

Many gamers complain about the lack of ludic play in Second Life and the 'lack of graphics'. They also tend to impose gaming tactics on Second Life activities. Gamers do use Second Life, but if used for educational purposes Second Life is generally not seen as a game. There is also often an assumption that 'technical people will inherently understand Second Life,' which is not always the case.

## That using Second Life in the same RL room will be easier than using it at a distance

It is not always easier to run it in a computer lab, but it can be a help when getting 'n00b' students familiar with Second Life on, for example, a blended programme. The main difficulties with using Second Life do not relate to where you are sitting but are to do with the Internet connection, the graphics card and computer specification. It might be easier to provide support tutorials with a group of students in a computer lab by wandering around the cohort, but after the initial orientation phase there is little advantage to this.

## That you have to learn the whole platform step by step

Although there are some tasks that are useful for students to learn, such as gestures and movement, putting on clothes, and moving and managing objects, it is often better to let students follow their motivations and initially learn through experience and experimenting. Fun activities can also help, for example my MSc student cohort at the University of Edinburgh was asked to buy an object in Second Life and sell it to the tutor for a profit. I didn't win, but learnt a lot in the process. The winner sold the tutor a rideable invisible yak.

## That an avatar that is not moving is not doing something

The overlaying of the notion of lurking that appears to have emerged as a negative position from virtual learning environments is not really relevant to Second Life. Watching, reflecting and waiting are all seen as acceptable avatar behaviours. Yet again what seems to occur is that there is an overlaying of practices that occur in discussion forums onto activities in Second Life. A somewhat poignant position is provided on this by Savin-Baden and Sinclair (2010) who suggest:

> there are further difficulties with the language of online learning. The notion of 'moderating' clearly locates the control with the lecturers. The notion of 'lurking' implies that silence and watching are inherently bad, whilst at the same time raising questions about what counts as presence in digital spaces – and who decides.
> (Savin-Baden and Sinclair, 2010)

## That it is easy to implement problem-based learning in Second Life

In designing my first Master's module using Second Life Problem-based learning (SL/PBL), I found there were particular complexities and challenges underlying learning in open/open source spaces. Such open spaces seem to be somewhat panoptical and although Bentham's (1787) original perspective was of a closed space and that the watched were unaware of the watcher, the openness and who is watching whom can be troublesome. For example, the watching in SL/PBL compared with face-to-face PBL is different: issues of communication, gestures, textual speak and bodily/avatar positioning and posturing are seen and watched differently. This 'watching differently' seems to be an interruption that might make learning in SL seem both smoother and more striated (following Deleuze and Guattari, 1988), than in face-to-face PBL. SL/PBL would seem to be a smooth *and* striated space since there is a sense of a learning trajectory, but it is also an important site of becoming. I had anticipated SL/PBL would have particular difficulties, but not as many or as complex as those I *did* experience, when I lead my first session during my MSc. It was not possible to facilitate this session as a PBL session because:

- I had not been able to prepare the participants as a PBL team
- It was a stand alone session with no genuine commitment to the task, each other or a further PBL seminar
- I had not anticipated that a stand alone session would be difficult to facilitate in a way that reflected a Freirian stance to facilitation and embraced dialogic learning. The consequence was that as a facilitator I intervened too much, did not prompt the team to work out their learning needs, or come up with a strategy
- The initial write up, in face-to-face sessions, of a strategy or a list of learning needs on paper or flip chart did not of course occur, and I had not anticipated that this might be problematic. It meant that the team did not focus their ideas or have anything to take away from the session.

As a result I reflected:

1) As a facilitator I did not know how to manage the PBL, so I need to rethink my role in a SL setting as being different from e-facilitation in PBL and face-to-face facilitation.[1]
2) I needed to prepare the PBL team well enough to manage SL/PBL seminars and ensure they understand their roles as students.[2] I will also need to develop some robust staff development to help staff manage this new facilitator role.

---

[1] Students in the seminar disagreed with the notion of SL as a panoptical space and I did not facilitate them effectively in locating the discussion in their own experiences or in exploring power in collaborative teams. They also wanted more background about the scenario which goes against the philosophy of PBL.

[2] One student dislikes SL and this is something I will need to take more account of.

3) One of the team members was present as an avatar but not interacting nor standing with the group. Although I had tried to contact her through instant messaging she did not respond. After the seminar she explained she had had to take a phone call from her director. What I learned was that I need to help students attending SL/PBL seminars to consider their commitment to the team.

4) There was too much writing on the screen and it was difficult to see and manage. It affected team interaction as they appeared distracted by having too much to read and concentrate on.

## Conclusion

To some extent the issues raised in this section would seem to suggest that teaching and learning in Second Life is complex, difficult and troublesome. This is not the case. Avoiding the mistakes mentioned above will make teaching in Second Life a more straightforward pleasure. However, what will also facilitate effective learning in Second Life is sound design of the space, the learning and the relationship between the teaching, learning and the environment.

# Glossary

**Aporia** (Greek: ἀπορία: *impasse; lack of resources; puzzlement; embarrassment*) is a puzzle or an impasse, but it can also denote the state of being perplexed, or at a loss, at such a puzzle or impasse.

**Augmented reality** – the live view of a physical world environment whose elements are merged with computer imagery, thus it places emphasis on the physical, so that information from virtual space is accessed from within physical space. An example of this would be the projection of Second Life into a physical space such as a real life conference.

**Augmented virtuality** – this is where the virtual space is augmented with aspects from physical space, so there is a sense of overlay between the two spaces.

**Avatar** – the bodily manifestation of one's self in the context of a 3D virtual world.

**Alt-avatar** – the creation of an alternative avatar to the one used on a more everyday basis. Often used by staff for social purposes, or to remain unnoticed by students if they are inworld and wish to be anonymous.

**Aura** – the area around and which bounds an object or person in a virtual world.

**Blogs (weblogs)** – personal websites consisting of regularly updated entries displayed in reverse chronological order. They may be used by learners in PBLonline to evidence their thinking openly to the rest of the team and the e-tutor.

**Bumping** – an aggressive act in Second Life of purposefully bumping into another avatar.

**Chatbots** – characters not controlled by a user within Second Life. The chatbots are also known as 'Non-Player Characters (NPCs)' that can be commanded to do certain actions by the facilitator, such as moving around.

**Cognitive ethnography** – an approach that explores the cognitive processes that affect the work carried out within a setting, whilst recognising in turn the effect that the material world and social context have on the actions carried out, and that the meanings attributed within the setting also affect the cognitive processes (Hollan et al., 2000).

**Conceptual or theoretical framework** – an existing concept or proven theory that serves to guide study design as well as interpretations.

**Connective ethnography** – this method is one of those that has stemmed from the argument of such researchers as Leander and McKim (2003), who have suggested the need to move beyond place-based ethnography. The central idea then is in combining online and offline ethnographic methodologies.

**Default avatar** – the general avatar that is used mostly for teaching in Second Life, as opposed to the Alt-avatar (as above).

**Embodiment** – the interaction of the body, material places and social spaces towards the development of meaning.

**Ethnography** – a systematic way of gathering data using qualitative methods, including participant observation, interviewing, the collection and analysis of various documents or artifacts, and individual narratives with a focus on the social environment, such as physical spaces, customs and culture.

**Flaming** – the sending of angry or inflammatory messages by email or group postings. It is considered bad netiquette.

**Freebie places** – places in Second Life where it is possible to pick up free clothes, articles and buildings, such as the Freebie Dungeon, Freebie warehouse and various junkyards.

**Griefers** – individuals who seem to enjoy causing others grief, such as bumping, hitting and generally being unpleasant, especially to newbies – may well be found at the Infohubs, Welcome Areas or Help Island Public.

**Group Scribbles** – software that allows students and staff to 'write' on sheets similar to Post-it® notes, and manage the movement of these electronic notes jointly within and between public and private spaces.

**Haptics** – the use of technology that creates a sense of touch, such as vibration or movement, in order to enhance visual engagement in immersive virtual worlds.

**Heads-up display, or HUD** – a display that presents data within Second Life without requiring the user to look away from his or her usual viewpoint. It is attached to a space, such as the ground, or an object, such as a tree, rather than an avatar.

**Holodecks** – changeable environments where the scene changes at the touch of a button. Originally developed as part of the StarTrek universe.

**Honesties** – the idea that there needs to be a sense that what counts as trustworthiness and truth is a negotiated position in research.

**HUD (Heads-up display)** – is a display that presents data within Second Life without requiring the user to look away from his or her usual viewpoint.

**Identity tourism** – a metaphor developed by Nakamura (2000) to portray identity appropriation in cyberspace. The advantage of such appropriation enables the possibility of playing with different identities without encountering the risk associated with racial difference in real life.

**Interpretivism** – the perspective that knowledge, contexts, meanings and ideas are a matter of interpretation, thus researchers analyse the meaning people confer upon their own and others' actions.

**Learning context** – the interplay of all the values, beliefs, relationships, frameworks and external structures that operate within a given learning environment.

**Learner identity** – an identity formulated through the interaction of learner and learning. The notion of learner identity moves beyond, but encapsulates the notion of learning style, and encompasses positions that students take up in learning situations, whether consciously or unconsciously.

**Limen/Liminal** – threshold, often referred to as a betwixt and between state.

**Liminality** – characterised by a stripping away of old identities and an oscillation between states, it is a betwixt and between state and there is a sense of being in a period of transition, often on the way to a new or different space.

**Linden Lab** – the maker of Second Life and the Second Life Grid, is a virtual world technology company.

**Linden dollars** – the currency used for buying and selling in Second Life. It is possible to convert them to US dollars and although exchange rates are relatively stable they do fluctuate. There are approximately 250 Linden dollars (L$) to the US dollar.

**Liquid learning** – characterised by emancipation, reflexivity and flexibility, so that knowledge and knowledge boundaries are contestable and always on the move.

**Lurking** – the action of reading chatroom discussions, group or message board postings, but not contributing.

**Machinima** – a word developed from a combination of *machine* and *cinema* – is the process of creating films in Second Life so that computer-generated imagery (CGI) is rendered using real-time, interactive 3D engines instead of professional 3D animation software.

**Meta-ethnography** – an approach to synthesizing and interpreting findings from multiple qualitative studies. Noblitt and Hare (1988), from the field of education, developed this interpretive approach which has served as the basis for most qualitative approaches to synthesising qualitative research.

**Meta-synthesis** – an approach to synthesis of qualitative studies (or qualitative and quantitative studies) that tends to be aggregative (as opposed to interpretive) in approach. However, the term is sometimes used interchangeably with meta-ethnography.

**Mini map** – this shows the layout of the land you are on, including buildings, with the round dot representing your avatar. It rotates as you turn and the green icons represent other avatars.

**MMORG** – Massively Multiplayer Online Role-playing Game. The focus in these games is on role play as opposed to MUVEs. The games tend to have some form of progression, social interaction within the game as well as in-game culture.

**Mixed reality** – is seen as a method for integrating virtual and physical spaces much more closely so that physical and digital objects co-exist and interact in real time.

**Moodle** – a free software e-learning platform designed to help educators create online courses. Its open source licence and modular design allows for global development.

**MUVE** – this refers to a multi-user virtual environment and is used to denote a difference between MMORGs that are games-related, and environments such as Second Life which are not usually seen as games. Thus a MUVE is seen as a more general reference to virtual worlds.

**Net generation** – the generation that has barely known a world without computers, the World Wide Web, highly interactive video games and mobile phones. For many of this generation instant messaging, rather than telephone or e-mail, is the primary form of communication.

**Newbie/Noob** – someone who has just arrived in Second Life, often wearing the standard jeans and T-shirt, who lacks the knowledge and movements of those already familiar with Second Life.

**Non-player characters (NPC)** – characters not controlled by a user within Second Life. The NPCs in this project are also known as 'chatbots' that can be commanded to do certain actions by the facilitator, such as moving around.

**Online tone** – hearing what is being 'said' in an online context, particularly in discussion forums, and being able to locate anger, distress and pleasure, without the use of emoticons. The ability to 'read' voices is something that needs to be developed by facilitators.

**Photorealism** – the original term refers to the genre of painting based on a photograph, but it is referred to in Second Life as the highly realistic reproduction of objects and buildings from real life.

**Place illusion** (Slater et al., 2009) – the type of presence that refers to the sense of 'being there' in spite of knowing that you are not.

**Plausibility** – a technique for ensuring rigour in qualitative research synthesis that involves locating the truths and the realities in a study, adopting a critical approach and acknowledging the complexities of managing 'truths' in research.

**Plausibility illusion** (Slater et al., 2009) – is defined as how the world is perceived. 'Psi is the illusion that what is apparently happening is really happening (even though you know for sure that it is not)' (p. 8).

**Podcast** – a digital media file, or a series of such files, that is distributed over the Internet.

**Positivism** – a philosophical system which recognises only positive facts and observable phenomena, thus the only reliable knowledge of any field of phenomena reduces to knowledge of particular instances of patterns. Therefore reality is single and tangible, research is value free and generalisations are possible.

**Posting** – (verb) to publish a message on an online forum or discussion group; (noun) a message published on an online forum or discussion group.

**Prims** – primitives or prims. Objects in Second Life are constructed out of these constituent parts termed 'prims'. There are 15 basic prim shapes (Cube, Prism, Pyramid, Tetrahedron, Cylinder, Hemicylinder, Cone, Hemicone, Sphere, Hemisphere, Torus, Tube, Ring) which can be rezzed from the Second Life building interface.

**Problem-based learning** – an approach to learning where the focus for learning is on problem situations, rather than content. Students work in small teams and are facilitated by a tutor.

**Problem-based learning team** – a number of students (4–10) who work together as a defined group to manage a problem-based learning scenario.

**Problem-solving learning** – teaching where the focus is on students solving a given problem by acquiring the answers expected by the lecturer, answers that are rooted in the information supplied in some way to the students. The solutions are bounded by the content and students are expected to explore little extra material other than that with which they have been provided, in order to discover the solutions.

**Problem-based Learning Online** – a generic term which captures that vast variety of ways in which problem-based learning is being used synchronously and asynchronously, on campus, or at a distance. It represents the idea that students learn through web-based materials including text, simulations, videos and demonstrations, and resources such as chatrooms, message boards and environments that have been purpose-built for problem-based learning.

**Proxemics** – the study of spatial distances between individuals in different cultures and situations.

**Qualia** – a term used in philosophy to describe the subjective quality of conscious experience. In virtual worlds it tends to be used to refer to the illusion and extent of being present in an environment.

**Qualitative research** – a term that describes a developing field of inquiry and covers several research approaches that share a set of common characteristics. Those who use the approach frequently seek to understand human behaviour. They often are interested in the 'why' and 'how' questions, rather than the 'what'. Data collected and presented generally is thick in its description.

**Qualitative research synthesis** – an approach for integrating information from existing qualitative studies (Major and Savin-Baden, 2010a).

**Reflexivity** – seeking to continually challenge our biases and examine our stances, perspectives and views as researchers. This is not meant to be a notion of 'situating oneself' as formulaic as pronouncing a particular positioned identity connected with class, gender or race ... but rather situating oneself in order to interpret data demands so as to engage with critical questions.

**Rez** – means to create or to make an object appear.

**'Rezzing** an object' – can be done by dragging it from a resident's inventory or by creating a new one via the edit window. The term rezzing can also be used for waiting for a texture or object to load, such as 'Everything is still rezzing'.

**Sandbox** – a special place where restrictions to building and scripting are either low or non-existent. This is done to allow residents to build items or test scripts without having to get in the way of other residents, and is often used as a space to try things out. Generally these spaces are cleared daily.

**Scaffolding** – the concept of scaffolding is based on Vygotsky's zone of proximal development (Vygotsky, 1978). Individualised support designed to facilitate a student's ability to build on prior knowledge and to generate and internalise new knowledge is provided by the tutor or other students. The support is pitched just beyond the current level of the student.

**Second Life** – a 3D virtual world created by Linden Lab set in an Internet-based world. Residents (in the forms of self-designed avatars) in this world interact with each other and can learn, socialise, participate in activities, and buy and sell items with one another.

**SLOODLE** (Simulation Linked Object Oriented Dynamic Learning Environment) brings together Second Life and the virtual learning environment Moodle. It comprises the product of SLOODLE as software; the SLOODLE community, a group of users and developers; and the research studies related to SLOODLE for academic and product development.

**Spatial interaction (model of)** – developed by Benford et al. (1993; 1994), it is a model that provides flexible support for managing conversation between groups and can be used to control interactions among other kinds of objects as well.

**Teleport** – transferring from one location to another in Second Life almost instantaneously, this can occur by being offered a teleport by another avatar or choosing to teleport yourself to a new location.

**Text chat** – the means of communicating in Second Life by typing a response to another avatar inworld.

**Threshold concept** – the idea of a portal that opens up a way of thinking that was previously inaccessible (Meyer and Land, 2003).

**Transition** – shifts in learner experience caused by a challenge to the person's life-world. Transitions occur in particular areas of students' lives, at different times and in distinct ways. The notion of transitions carries with it the idea of movement from one place to another and with it the necessity of taking up a new position in a different place.

**Transitional learning** – learning that occurs as a result of critical reflection upon shifts (transitions) that have taken place for the students personally (including viscerally), pedagogically and/or interactionally.

**Troublesome knowledge** – Perkins (1999) described conceptually difficult knowledge as 'troublesome knowledge'. This is knowledge that appears, for example, counter intuitive, alien (emanating from another culture or discourse), or incoherent (discrete aspects are unproblematic but there is no organising principle).

**Troublesome spaces** – places where 'stuckness' or 'disjunction' occurs.

**Viral methodologies** – instead of research methodologies being specifically 'located' in areas such as post-structuralism and constructivism, the underlying theories are seen as mutable and liquid.

**Virtual ethnography** – methodology that seeks to understand, from a sociological perspective, what people 'do' on the Internet (Hine, 2000).

**Virtual learning environment (VLE)** – a set of learning and teaching tools involving online technology designed to enhance students' learning experience, for example, Blackboard, WebCT.

**Virtual patients** – simulations or representations of individuals who are designed by facilitators as a means of creating a character in a health care setting.

**Virtual reality** – a simulated computer environment in an either real or imaginary world. Most virtual reality emphasises immersion, so that the user suspends belief and accepts it as a real environment and uses head mounted displays to enhance this.

**Web 2.0 technologies** – now a somewhat dated term, but refers to the development of social software such as a wiki or blogs, which have become user driven and facilitate information sharing and social networking.

**Webinars** – conducting live meetings, seminars or presentations via the Internet.

**Weblip** – an instant messaging system that aims to connect you to other Weblip users currently viewing the same website. Rather than using a chat window, it uses an overlaying animated avatar that stands at the bottom of the browser's window.

**Wikis** – server software that allows multiple users to contribute to, and edit web page content.

**World of Warcraft** – a highly popular massively multiplayer online role-playing game (MMORPG) developed by Blizzard Entertainment. Players control an avatar to explore locations, defeat creatures and complete quests. The game is set in the world of Azeroth.

# Weblinks

## Introduction

Viewer 2 http://secondlife.com/beta-viewer/

## Chapter 1 The value of Second Life for learning in higher education

Viewer 2 http://secondlife.com/beta-viewer/

## Chapter 2 Practical tips for getting started

Vassar Island http://maps.secondlife.com/secondlife/Vassar/128/128/0/
Ancient Rome http://maps.secondlife.com/secondlife/ROMA/128/128/0/
NMC Orientation island http://slurl.com/secondlife/NMC%20
   Orientation/69/107/32/.
NMC's Web site http://sl.nmc.org/create.php
The National Workshop on Learning in Immersive Virtual Worlds
   http://cuba.coventry.ac.uk/learninginnovation/national-workshop-
   registration/national-workshop-2009/
Second Life Educators https://lists.secondlife.com/cgi-bin/mailman/
   listinfo/educators
Second Life Research Listserv http://list.academ-x.com/listinfo.cgi/
   slrl-academ-x.com
JISC Regional Support Centres http://www.jisc.ac.uk/whatwedo.aspx
Daden http://www.daden.co.uk/
CitrusVirtual http://www.citrusvirtual.com/
solution providers in Second Life http://solutionproviders.secondlife.
   com/
create property lines http://wiki.secondlife.com/wiki/Private_Island#
   Creating_Property_Lines
Second Life Wiki http://wiki.secondlife.com/wiki/Main_Page
part-time employees http://foo.secondlifeherald.com/slh/2008/05/irs-
   rules-in-wo.html
OpenSim http://opensimulator.org/wiki/Main_Page

Project Wonderland http://www.projectwonderland.com/
Mirtle http://research.sun.com/techrep/2009/smli_tr-2009-182.pdf
ActiveWorlds http://www.activeworlds.com/
Twinity http://www.twinity.com/en
Blue Mars http://www.bluemarsonline.com/
Avatar Reality http://www.avatar-reality.com/
Web.alive http://avayalive.com/WaStore/
Schome Park project. http://www.schome.ac.uk/
Club Penguin http://clubpenguin.com/
Habbo http://www.habbo.co.uk/

## Chapter 3 Planning and designing learning in Second Life

fablusi http://www.fablusi.com/
unigame http://unigame.net/
PREVIEW http://www.elu.sgul.ac.uk/preview/blog/
   developing machinima http://wiki.secondlife.com/wiki/Video_
   Tutorials#Machinima
providing tutorials http://wiki.secondlife.com/wiki/Video_Tutorials#
   Official_Video_Tutorials

## Chapter 4 Teaching approaches to use in Second Life

Echo 360 http://www.echo360.com/
video streaming http://wiki.secondlife.com/wiki/Play_media
AngryBeth's Whiteboard http://angrybethshortbread.blogspot.com/
   2006/05/inworld-interactive-whiteboard_19.html
Giving a PowerPoint Presentation in Second Life
http://sl.nmc.org/wiki/Getting_a_PowerPoint_Presentation_into_Second_
   Life
Viewer 2 http://secondlife.com/beta-viewer/
GoogleDocs http://docs.google.com/
SlideShare http://www.slideshare.net/
HERMES http://bufvc.ac.uk/oldwebsite/databases/index.html
Streaming video into Second Life http://www.aiai.ed.ac.uk/project/
   i-room/vc/resources/Streaming-Video-to-from-SL.pdf
Medical Education Technologies Inc http://www.meti.com/
Imperial College School of Medicine http://www1.imperial.ac.uk/
   medicine/research/researchthemes/healthtechnologies/simulation/
   mmdl/

uploading audio http://wiki.secondlife.com/wiki/Help:Streaming_Audio
PREVIEW YouTube channel http://www.youtube.com/user/
  PreviewProject
pandorabot http://www.pandorabots.com/botmaster/en/home

## Chapter 5  Purposeful pedagogy

Open Habitat http://openhabitat.net/
Sounds Good http://sites.google.com/site/soundsgooduk/
Awesome http://awesome.leeds.ac.uk/

## Chapter 7  Equipping students for learning in Second Life

Weblip http://www.weblip.com/home.php
JISC Second Life Guide http://www.jisc.ae.uk/news/stories/2009/08/
  secondlife.aspx
Sloodle Tracker http://www.ics.heacademy.ac.uk/italics/.../ItalicsVol8Iss
  3Nov2009Paper01.pdf

## Chapter 8  Assessment for learning in Second Life

Effective Practice with e-Assessment http://www.jisc.ac.uk/publications
  /.../2007/pub_eassesspracticeguide.aspx
80 Days project http://www.eightydays.eu/

## Chapter 9  Harnessing technology for learning

SLOODLE (Simulation Linked Object Oriented Dynamic Learning
  Environment). http://www.sloodle.org/
PIVOTE virtual learning authoring system for virtual worlds
  http://www.pivote.info/
JISC http://www.jisc.ac.uk/
PREVIEW http://www.elu.sgul.ac.uk/preview/blog/
Medbiquitous Virtual Patient http://www.medbiq.org/working_groups/
  virtual_patient/index.html
PIVOTE Information Centre in Second Life http://slurl.com/secondlife/
  St%20Georges%20University/123/16/21

video tutorials on YouTube http://www.youtube.com/watch?v=
  81c0y3JngiQ
Introduction to PIVOTE http://pivote.googlecode.com/files/
  Introduction%20to%20PIVOTE%200a.pdf
PIVOTE Overview http://pivote.googlecode.com/files/PIVOTE%
  20Overview.pdf
Google Code site. http://code.google.com/p/pivote/
ICOPER Interoperable Content for Performance in a Competency-driven
  Society http://www.icoper.org/
XDELIA Xcellence in Decision-making through Enhanced Learning in
  Immersive Applications http://www.xdelia.org/
COSPATIAL Communication and Social Participation: collaborative Tech-
  nologies for Interaction and Learning http://cospatial.fbk.eu/
eCIRCUS Education Through Characters With Emotional-Intelligence
  And Roleplaying Capabilities That Understand Social Interaction
  http://www.macs.hw.ac.uk/EcircusWeb/
COOPER Collaborative Open Environment for Project-Centred Learning
  http://www.cooper-project.org/
GRAPPLE project Generic Responsive Adaptive Personalized Learning
  Environment. http://www.grapple-project.org/
<e-Adventure> http://e-adventure.e-ucw.es/
ELEKTRA Enhanced Learning Experience and Knowledge Transfer
  http://www.elektra-project.org/
80 Days http://www.eightydays.eu/
VICTEC project Virtual ICT with Empathic Characters
  http://www.macs.hw.ac.uk/victec/index_geral.html

## Chapter 10  Researching immersive virtual worlds

Participatory Pattern Workshop methodology
http://patternlanguagenetwork.myxwiki.org/xwiki/bin/view/Patterns/
  ParticipatoryPatternWorkshops
viral learning (see for example, Downes) http://www.downes.ca/
  cgi-bin/page.cgi

## Chapter 11  Futures and possibilities

Wikitude World Browser http://www.wikitude.org/world_browser
realXtend http://www.realxtend.org/
Facegen's photofit http://www.cybertechnews.org/?p=34

Ludocraft http://www.ludocraft.com/
face tracking and facial animation http://n2.nabble.com/-realXtend–
   facial-animation-td2508826.html

## Appendix A  Second Life: module exemplar

www.secondlife.com

## Appendix B  Dealing with challenges and mistakes in Second Life

PIVOTE http://www.pivote.info/

# References

Addison, A. and O'Hare, L. (2008) How can massive multi-user virtual environments and virtual role play enhance traditional teaching practice?, in *Proceedings of ReLIVE08 Conference*, Milton Keynes, 20–21 November (available at: www.open.ac.uk/relive08/).

Alexander, C. (1979) *The Timeless Way of Building*. New York: Oxford University Press.

Alexander, C., Ishikawa, S., Silverstein, M., Jacobson, M., Fiksdahl-King, I. and Angel, S. (1977) *A Pattern Language: Towns, Buildings, Construction*. New York: Oxford University Press.

Ausubel, D.P., Novak, J.S. and Hanesian, H. (1978) *Educational Psychology: A Cognitive View*. New York: Holt, Rinehart & Winston.

Barab, S., Dodge, T., Tuzun, H., Job-Sluder, K., Jackson, C., Arici, A., Job-Sluder, L. et al. (2007) The Quest Atlantis Project: a socially-responsive play space for learning, in B.E. Shelton and D. Wiley (eds.) *The Educational Design and Use of Simulation Computer Games*. Rotterdam: Sense Publishers.

Bardzell, S. and Odom, W. (2008) The experience of embodied space in virtual worlds: an ethnography of a Second Life community, *Space and Culture: An International Journal of Social Spaces*, 11(3): 239–259.

Barnett, R. (1997) *Higher Education: A Critical Business*. Buckingham: Open University Press/SRHE.

Barnett, R. (2000) *Realizing the University in an Age of Supercomplexity*. Buckingham: Open University Press/SRHE.

Barnett, R. and Coate, K. (2005) *Engaging the Curriculum in Higher Education*. Maidenhead: McGraw-Hill.

Barr, R.B. and Tagg, J. (1995) From teaching to learning – a new paradigm for undergraduate education, *Change Magazine*, 27(6): 12–25.

Barrows, H.S. and Tamblyn, R.M. (1980) *Problem-Based Learning: An Approach to Medical Education*. New York: Springer.

Bauman, Z. (2000) *Liquid Modernity*. Cambridge: Polity Press.

Bayne, S. (2008) Higher education as a visual practice: seeing through the virtual learning environment, *Teaching in Higher Education*, 13(4): 395–410.

Becher, T. and Trowler, P. (2001) *Academic Tribes and Territories: Intellectual Enquiry and The Culture of Disciplines* (2nd edn.). Buckingham: Open University Press/SRHE.

Beer, M., Slack, F. and Armitt, G. (2003) Community building and virtual teamwork in an online learning environment, in *Proceedings of the 36th Annual Hawaii International Conference on System Sciences* (Track 1). Los Alamitos, CA: IEEE Computer Society.

Benford, S. (2009) Hybrid spatial structure in ubiquitous computing, a short paper for the *Bigraphs Workshop*, first draft, June 2009 (http://www.mrl.nott.ac.uk/~sdb/research/bigraphsworkshop/hybrid%20spatial%20structure.pdf).

Benford, S.D. and Fahlén, L.E. (1993) A spatial model of interaction in virtual environments, in G. De Michelis, C. Simone and K. Schmidt (eds.) *Proceedings of the European Conference on Computer Supported Co-operative Work*. Amsterdam: Kluwer Academic.

Benford, S., Bowers, J., Fahlén, L.E. and Greenhalgh, C. (1994) Managing mutual awareness in collaborative virtual environments, in *Proceedings of the First Conference on Virtual Reality Software and Technology*, Singapore.

Benford, S., Bowers, J., Fahlén, L., Greenhalgh, C. and Snowdon, D. (1995) User embodiment in collaborative virtual environments, in *Proceedings of ACM Conference on Human Factors in Computing Systems*. New York: ACM Press.

Bentham, J. (1787/1995) *The Panopticon Writings* (ed. M. Bozovic). London: Verso (accessed 18 October 2007 at: http://cartome.org/panopticon2.htm).

Bernstein, B. (1992) Pedagogic identities and educational reform, paper presented to Santiago conference, Mimeo.

Birenbaum, M. (1997). Assessment preferences and their relationship to learning strategies and orientations, *Higher Education*, 33: 71–84.

Black, R.W. and Steinkuehler, C. (2009) Literacy in virtual worlds, in L. Christenbury, R. Bomer and P. Smagorinsky (eds.) *Handbook of Adolescent Literacy Research*. New York: Guilford Press.

Bloomfield, P.R. and Livingstone, D. (2009) Immersive learning and assessment with quizHUD, *Computing and Information Systems Journal*, 13(1).

Boardman, K. (2009) Dreams into [virtual] reality, paper presented at the *16th International Conference of the Association for Learning Technology: In Dreams Begins Responsibility – Choice, Evidence, and Change*, Manchester, 8–10 September.

Boostrom, R. (2008) The social construction of virtual reality and the stigmatized identity of the newbie, *Journal of Virtual Worlds Research*, 1(2): 1–19.

Boud, D. (1995) Assessment and learning: contradictory or complementary?, in P. Knight (ed.) *Assessment for Learning in Higher Education*. London: Kogan Page.

Bovill, C., Morss, K. and Bulley, C. (2009) Should students participate in curriculum design? Discussion arising from a first year curriculum design project and a literature review, *PRIME*, 3(2): 17–26.

Brown, A.L. (1992). Design experiments: theoretical and methodological challenges in creating complex interventions in classroom settings, *Journal of the Learning Sciences*, 2(2): 141–178.

Brown, E., Gordon, M. and Hobbs, M. (2008) Second Life as a holistic learning environment for problem-based learning and transferable skills, in *Proceedings of ReLIVE08 Conference*, Milton Keynes, 20–21 November (available at: www.open.ac.uk/relive08/).

Brown, G. and Atkins, M. (2002) *Effective Teaching in Higher Education*. London: Routledge.

Bruner, J. (1991) *Acts of Meaning*. Cambridge, MA: Harvard University Press.

Callaghan, M.J., McCusker, K., Lopez Losada, J., Harkin, J.G. and Wilson, S. (2009) Engineering Education Island: teaching engineering in virtual worlds, *ITALICS*, 8(3): 2–18.

Camilleri, V. and Montebello, M. (2008) SLAVE – Second Life Assistant in a Virtual Environment, in *Proceedings of ReLIVE08 Conference*, Milton Keynes, 20–21 November (available at: www.open.ac.uk/relive08/).

Carr, D. (2010) Constructing disability in online worlds: conceptualising disability in online research, *London Review of Education: Special Issue on 'Being Online: A Critical View of Identity and Subjectivity in New Virtual Learning Spaces'*.

Carr, D. and Oliver, M. (2009) Second Life, immersion and learning, in P. Zaphiris and Chee Siang Ang (eds.) *Social Computing and Virtual Communities*. London: Chapman & Hall.

Celentano, A. and Pittarello, F. (2004) Observing and adapting user behaviour in navigational 3D interface, in *Proceedings of the 7th International Conference on Advanced Visual Interfaces*. New York: ACM Press.

Chafer, J. and Childs, M. (2008) The impact of the characteristics of a virtual performance: concepts, constraints and complications, in *Proceedings of ReLIVE08 Conference*, Milton Keynes, 20–21 November (available at: www.open.ac.uk/relive08/).

Chittaro, L. and Ranon, R. (2000) Adding adaptive features to virtual reality interfaces for e-commerce, in *Proceedings of the First International Conference on Adaptive Hypermedia and Adaptive Web-based Systems*. Lecture Notes in Computer Science #1892. Berlin: Springer.

Chittaro, L. and Ranon, R. (2007) Adaptive hypermedia techniques for 3D educational virtual environments, *IEEE Intelligent Systems*, 22(4): 31–37.

Chittaro, L. and Ranon, R. (2008). An adaptive 3D virtual environment for learning the X3D language, in *Proceedings of the 2008 International Conference on Intelligent User Interfaces*. New York: ACM Press.

Coleridge, S.T (1817/1983) *Biographia Literaria*. Princeton, NJ: Princeton University Press.

Collins, A. (1992) Towards a design science of education, in E. Scanlon and T. O'Shea (eds.) *New Directions in Educational Technology* (pp. 15–22). Berlin: Springer.

Conradi, E., Kavia, S., Burden, D., Rice, D., Woodham, L., Beaumont, C. et al. (2009) Virtual patients in a virtual world: training paramedic students for practice, *Medical Teacher*, 31(8): 713–720.

Corbyn, Z. (2009) Second Life out as techies embrace cloud email, *Times Higher Education*, 20 August (http://www.timeshighereducation. co.uk/story.asp?storycode=407839).

Cormier, D. (2009) MUVE eventedness – an experience like any other, *British Journal of Educational Technology*, 40(3): 543–546.

Dean, E., Cook, S., Keating, M. and Murphy, J. (2009) Does this avatar make me look fat? Obesity and interviewing in Second Life, *Journal of Virtual Worlds Research*, 2(2): 3–11.

Dede, C. (1995) The evolution of constructivist learning environments: immersion in distributed, virtual worlds, *Educational Technology*, 35(5): 46–52.

Dede, C. (2009) Immersive interfaces for engagement and learning, *Science*, 323(5910): 66–69.

Deleuze, G. and Guattari, F. (1988) *A Thousand Plateaus: Capitalism and Schizophrenia*. London: Continuum.

De Pascale, M., Mulatto, S. and Prattichizzo, D. (2008) Bringing haptics to Second Life for visually impaired people, in *Proceedings of the 2008 Ambi-Sys Workshop on Haptic User Interfaces in Ambient Media Systems*, 11–14 February, Quebec City, Quebec.

Dervin, B. (1998) Sense-making theory and practice: an overview of user interests in knowledge seeking and use, *Journal of Knowledge Management*, 2(2): 36–46.

Design-Based Research Collective (2003) Design-based research: an emerging paradigm for educational inquiry, *Educational Researcher*, 32(1): 5–8.

De Troyer, O., Kleinermann, F., Pellens, B. and Ewais, A. (2009) Supporting virtual reality in an adaptive web-based learning environment: learning in the synergy of multiple disciplines, in U. Cress, V. Dimitrova and M. Specht (eds.) *Proceedings of the 4th European Conference on Technology Enhanced Learning (EC-TEL)*. Lecture Notes in Computer Science #5794. Berlin: Springer.

Dewey, J. (1938) *Experience and Education*. New York: Collier & Kappa Delta Pi.

Ducheneaut, N., Wen, M., Yee, N. and Wadley, G. (2009) Body and mind: a study of avatar personalization in three virtual worlds, in *Proceedings of the 27th Annual CHI Conference on Human Factors in Computing Systems*, 4–9 April, Boston, MA.

Duncan, M. and Watson, R. (2010) Taking a stance: socially responsible ethics and informed consent, in M. Savin-Baden and C. Major (eds.) *New Approaches to Qualitative Research: Wisdom and Uncertainty*. London: Routledge.

Durand, F. (2002) An invitation to discuss computer depiction, in *Proceedings of the Second International Symposium on Nonphotorealistic Animation and Rendering*. New York: ACM Press.

Eva, K.W., Neville, A.J. and Norman, G.R. (1998) Exploring the etiology and content specificity: factors influencing analogic transfer and problem solving, *Academic Medicine*, 73: S1–S5.

Finlay, J., Gray, J., Falconer, I., Hensman, J., Mor, I. and Warburton, S. (2009) *PLaNet: Pattern Language Network for Web 2.0 in Learning*. Final Report. Bristol: JISC.

Flecha, R. (2000) *Sharing Words: Theory and Practice of Dialogic Learning*. Lanham, MA: Rowman & Littlefield.

Foucault, M. (1975) *Discipline and Punish: The Birth of the Prison* (trans. A. Sheridan 1977). London: Penguin Books.

Freire, P. (1972) *Pedagogy of the Oppressed*. London: Penguin Books.

Freire, P. (1974) *Education: The Practice of Freedom*. London: Writers & Readers Cooperative.

Galas, C. and Ketelhut, D.J. (2006) River City, the MUVE, *Leading and Learning with Technology*, 33(7): 31–32.

Gee, J.P. (2004) *What Video Games Have to Teach Us about Learning and Literacy*. Basingstoke: Palgrave Macmillan.

Geertz, C. (1973) *The Interpretation of Cultures*. New York: Basic Books.

Gibson, E.J. and Walk, R.D. (1960) The 'visual cliff', *Scientific American*, 202(4): 67–71.

Gilleade, K.M. and Dix, A. (2004) Using frustration in the design of adaptive videogames, in *Proceedings of the 2004 ACM SIGCHI International Conference on Advances in Computer Entertainment Technology*. New York: ACM Press.

Gillen, J. (2009) Literacy practices in Schome Park: a virtual literacy ethnography, *Journal of Research in Reading*, 32(1): 55–74.

Glover, C. and Brown, E. (2006) Written feedback for students: too much or too incomprehensible to be effective?, *Bioscience Education e-Journal*, 7(3) (available at: http://www.bioscience.heacademy.ac.uk/journal/vol7/beej-7-3.aspx).

Goffman, E. (1963) *Stigma: Notes on the Management of Spoiled Identity*. Englewood Cliffs, NJ: Prentice-Hall.

Goodfellow, R. and Lea, M. (2005) Supporting writing for assessment in online learning, *Assessment and Evaluation in Higher Education*, 30(3): 261–271.

Gutiérrez, K., Baquedano-Lopez, P. and Tejeda, C. (1999) Rethinking diversity: hybridity and hybrid language practices in the third space, *Mind, Culture, and Activity: An International Journal*, 6(4): 286–303.

Haggis, T. (2004) Meaning, identity and 'motivation': expanding what matters in understanding learning in higher education?, *Studies in Higher Education*, 29(3): 335–352.

Haggis, T. (2006) Pedagogies for diversity: retaining critical challenge amidst fears of 'dumbing down', *Studies in Higher Education*, 31(5): 521–535.

Hall, S. (1996) Introduction: who needs 'identity'?, in S. Hall and P. du Gay (eds.) *Questions of Cultural Identity*. London: Sage.

Hayles, K. (1999) *How We Became Posthuman: Virtual Bodies in Cybernetics, Literature and Informatics*. Chicago, IL: University of Chicago Press.

Heidegger, M. (1985). *Being and Time*. Oxford: Basil Blackwell.

Heron, J. (1989) *The Facilitator's Handbook*. London: Kogan Page.

Heron, J. (1993) *Group Facilitation*. London: Kogan Page.

Hemmi, A., Bayne, S. and Land, R. (2009) The appropriation and repurposing of social technologies in higher education, *Journal of Computer Assisted Learning*, 25(1): 19–30.

Herrington, J., Oliver, R. and Reeves, T.C. (2003) Patterns of engagement in authentic online learning environments, *Australian Journal of Educational Technology*, 19(1): 59–71.

Hine, C. (2000). *Virtual Ethnography*. London: Sage.

Hine, C. (2007) Connective ethnography for the exploration of e-science, *Journal of Computer-Mediated Communication*, 12(2) (available at: http://jcmc.indiana.edu/vol12/issue2/hine.html).

Hollan, J., Hutchins, E. and Kirsh, D. (2000) Distributed cognition: toward a new foundation for human–computer interaction research, *ACM Transactions on Computer–Human Interaction*, 7(2): 174–196.

hooks, B. (1994) *Teaching to Transgress*. London: Routledge.

Hounsell, D. (2008) The trouble with feedback: new challenges, emerging strategies, *TLA Interexchange*, 2: 1–10.

Hounsell, D., Falchikov, N., Hounsell, J., Klampfleitner, M., Huxham, M., Thomson, K. et al. (2007) *Innovative Assessment across the Disciplines: An Analytical Review of the Literature*. York: Higher Education Academy.

Jeffery, C. (2008) Using non-player characters as tutors in virtual environments, in *Proceedings of ReLIVE08 Conference*, Milton Keynes, 20–21 November (available at: www.open.ac.uk/relive08/).

Jenkins, A. and Zetter, R. (2003) *Linking Teaching and Research in Departments*. York: Higher Education Academy.

JISC (2007) *Effective Practice with e-Assessment: An Overview of Technologies, Policies and Practice in Further and Higher Education.* Bristol: JISC.

Johnson, D.W., Johnson, R.T. and Smith, K.A. (1991) *Cooperative Learning: Increasing College Faculty Instructional Productivity.* ASHE-ERIC Higher Education Report #4. Washington, DC: The George Washington University, School of Education and Social Development.

Johnson, D.W., Johnson, R.T. and Smith, K.A. (1998) *Active Learning: Cooperation in the College Classroom.* Edina, MN: Interaction Book Company.

Kang, M., Kim, J. and Park, M. (2008) Investigating presence as a predictor of learning outcomes in e-learning environment, in *Proceedings of World Conference on Educational Multimedia, Hypermedia and Telecommunications 2008.* Chesapeake, VA: AACE (http://www.editlib.org/p/28965).

Kemp, J., Livingstone, D. and Bloomfield, P.R. (2009) SLOODLE: connecting VLE tools with emergent teaching practice in Second Life, *British Journal of Educational Technology*, 40(3): 551–555.

Kinchin, I.M., Cabot, L.B. and Hay, D.B. (2008) Visualising expertise: revealing the nature of a threshold concept in the development of an authentic pedagogy for clinical education, paper presented to the *Threshold Concepts Symposium*, Kingston, Ontario, 18–20 June.

Knight, P.T. (2001) *A Briefing on Key Concepts: Formative and Summative, Criterion and Norm-referenced Assessment.* LTSN Generic Centre Assessment Series #7. York: LTSN.

Kolb, D.A. and Fry, R. (1975) Towards an applied theory of experiential learning, in C.L. Cooper (ed.) *Theories of Group Processes.* Chichester: Wiley.

Land, R., Meyer, J.H.F. and Smith, J. (eds.) (2008) *Threshold Concepts within the Disciplines.* Rotterdam: Sense Publishers.

Laurillard, D. (2002) *Rethinking University Teaching: A Conversational Framework for the Effective Use of Learning Technologies.* London: Routledge.

Lea, M. (2001) Computer conferencing and assessment: new ways of writing in higher education, *Studies in Higher Education*, 26(2): 163–181.

Leander, K.M. and McKim, K.K. (2003) Tracing the everyday 'sitings' of adolescents on the Internet: a strategic adaptation of ethnography across online and offline spaces, *Education, Communication and Information*, 3(2): 211–240.

Lewis, C.S. (1940) *The Problem of Pain.* London: HarperCollins.

Lincoln, Y. and Guba, E. (1985) *Naturalistic Inquiry.* London: Sage.

Livingstone, D. and Kemp, J. (2008) Mixed-methods and mixed-worlds: engaging globally distributed user groups for extended evaluation studies, in *Proceedings of ReLIVE08 Conference*, Milton Keynes, 20–21 November (available at: www.open.ac.uk/relive08/).

Lowe, S. (2003) Embodied space(s): anthropological theories of body, space, and culture, *Space and Culture*, 6: 9–18 (http://sac.sagepub.com/cgi/content/abstract/6/1/9).

Macfarlane, B. (2010) Values and virtues in qualitative research, in M. Savin-Baden and C. Major (eds.) *New Approaches to Qualitative Research: Wisdom and Uncertainty*. London: Routledge.

Major, C. and Savin-Baden, M. (2010a) *An Introduction to Qualitative Research Synthesis: Managing the Information Explosion in Social Science Research*. London: Routledge.

Major, C. and Savin-Baden, M. (2010b) Qualitative research synthesis: the scholarship of integration in practice, in M. Savin-Baden and C. Major (eds.) *New Approaches to Qualitative Research: Wisdom and Uncertainty*. London: Routledge.

Malaby, T. (2006) Parlaying value: capital in and beyond virtual worlds, *Games and Culture*, 1(2): 141–162.

Marton, F. and Säljö, R. (1976a) On qualitative differences in learning: I. Outcome and process, *British Journal of Educational Psychology*, 46: 4–11.

Marton, F. and Säljö, R. (1976b) On qualitative differences in learning: II. Outcome as a function of the learner's conception of the task, *British Journal of Educational Psychology*, 46: 115–127.

Mason, H. and Moutahir, M. (2006) Multidisciplinary experiential education in Second Life: a global approach, in D. Livingstone and J. Kemp (eds.) *Proceedings of the Second Life Education Workshop*. Paisley: University of Paisley (available at: http://www.simteach.com/SLCC06/).

Mayes, T. and De Freitas, S. (2004) *Stage 2: Review of e-Learning Theories, Frameworks and Models*. Colchester: University of Essex (accessed 15 April 2009 at: http://www.essex.ac.uk/chimera/projects/jisc/Stage%202%20Learning%20Models%20(Version%201).pdf).

McDowell, L., Sambell, K. and Jessop, A. (2008) Assessment for learning: a brief history and review of terminology, in *Proceedings of the 16th Improving Student Learning Symposium: Improving Student Learning – Through the Curriculum*. Oxford: Oxford Centre for Staff and Learning Development.

McKenna, C. and McAvinia, C. (2007) Difference and discontinuity – making meaning though hypertexts, paper presented at *Ideas in Cyberspace Education 3*, Loch Lomond, 21–23 March (accessed 4 April at: www.education.ed.ac.uk/ice3/papers).

Meltzoff, A.N. (1995) Understanding the intentions of others: re-enactment of intended acts by 18-month-old children, *Developmental Psychology*, 31: 838–850.

Meltzoff, A.N. (2007) The 'like me' framework for recognizing and becoming an intentional agent, *Acta Psychologica*, 124: 26–43.

Meltzoff, A.N., Kuhl, P., Movellan, J. and Sejnowski, T.J. (2009) Foundations for a new science of learning, *Science*, 325(5938): 284–288.

Mercer, N. (1996) English at work, in J. Maybin and N. Mercer (eds.) *Using English: From Conversation to Canon*. London: Routledge.

Meyer, J.H.F. and Eley, M.G. (2006) The Approaches to Teaching Inventory: a critique of its development and applicability, *British Journal of Education Psychology*, 76: 633–649.

Meyer, J.H.F. and Land, R. (2003) Threshold concepts and troublesome knowledge (1): linkages to ways of thinking and practising within the disciplines, in C. Rust (ed.) *Improving Student Learning: Theory and Practice – 10 Years On*. Oxford: Oxford Centre for Staff and Learning Development.

Meyer, J. and Land, R. (2005) Threshold concepts and troublesome knowledge (2): epistemological considerations and a conceptual framework for teaching and learning, *Higher Education*, 49(3): 373–388.

Meyer, J.H.F. and Land, R. (2006) Threshold concepts and troublesome knowledge: issues of liminality, in J.H.F. Meyer and R. Land (eds.) *Overcoming Barriers to Student Understanding: Threshold Concepts and Troublesome Knowledge*. Abingdon: RoutledgeFalmer.

Meyer, J.H.F., Land, R. and Davies, P. (2008) Threshold concepts and troublesome knowledge (4): issues of variation and variability, in R. Land, J.H.F. Meyer and J. Smith (eds.) *Threshold Concepts within the Disciplines*. Rotterdam: Sense Publishers.

Mezirow, J. (1981) A critical theory of adult learning and education, *Adult Education*, 32(1): 3–24.

Mezirow, J. (1985) A critical theory of self-directed learning, in S. Brookfield (ed.) *Self-Directed Learning: From Theory to Practice*. San Francisco, CA: Jossey-Bass.

Milgram, P. and Kishino, F. (1994) A taxonomy of mixed reality visual displays, *IEICE Transactions on Information Systems*, E77-D12: 449–455.

Moody, L., Waterworth, W. and Zivanovic, A. (forthcoming) A desktop virtual environment for arthroscopy: achieving a suitable level of immersion, *Virtual Reality: Special Issue on Interaction and Usability Issues for Desktop Environments*.

Moreno-Ger, P., Blesisu, C., Currier, P., Sierra-Rodriguez, J.L. and Baltsar, F. (2008a) Online learning and clinical procedures: rapid development and effective deployment of game-like interactive simulations, in Z. Pan, D.A.D. Cheok, A.D. Müller and A. El Rhalibi (eds.) *Transactions on Edutainment I*. Lecture Notes in Computer Science #5080. Heidelberg: Springer.

Moreno-Ger, P., Sierra-Rodriguez, J.L. and Fernandez-Manjon, B. (2008b) Games-based learning in e-learning environments, *UPGRADE*, 12(3): 15–20.

Nakamura, L. (2000) *Race In/For Cyberspace: Identity Tourism and Racial Passing on the Internet* (accessed 30 October 2007 at: http://www.humanities.uci.edu/mposter/syllabi/readings/nakamura.html).

Nicol, D. (2008) Assessment as a driver for transformational change in HE, *ESCalate Newsletter*, 10 (spring) (accessed 2 June 2008 at: http://escalate.ac.uk/4451).

Noblit, G.W. and Hare, R.D. (1988) *Meta-ethnography: Synthesizing Qualitative Studies*. Newbury Park, CA: Sage.

Nystrand, M. (ed.) (1982) *What Writers Know: The Language, Process, and Structure of Written Discourse*. New York: Academic Press.

Olsen, S.F., Jensen, S.S., Bolander, K., Deepwell, F., Jones, C. and Mann, S. (2004) Narratives from the 3D Agora-world, in *Proceedings of the Networked Learning Conference*, Lancaster (available at: http://www.networkedlearningconference.org.uk/past/nlc2004/proceedings/individual_papers/olsen_et_al.htm).

Pausch, R., Proffitt, D. and Williams, G. (1997) Quantifying immersion in virtual reality, in *Proceedings of the 24th Annual Conference on Computer Graphics and Interactive Techniques*. New York: ACM Press/Addison Wesley.

Perkins, D. (1999) The many faces of constructivism, *Educational Leadership*, 57(3): 6–11.

Perkins, D. (2006a) Beyond understanding, keynote paper presented to the *Threshold Concepts in the Disciplines Symposium*, Strathclyde, 30 August.

Perkins, D. (2006b) Constructivism and troublesome knowledge, in J.H.F. Meyer and R. Land (eds.) *Overcoming Barriers to Student Understanding: Threshold Concepts and Troublesome Knowledge*. Abingdon: Routledge-Falmer.

Pirolli, P. (2007) *Information Foraging Theory: Adaptive Interaction with Information*. Oxford: Oxford University Press.

Porter, J. (1992) *Audience and Rhetoric: An Archaeological Composition of the Discourse Community*. Englewood Cliffs, NJ: Prentice-Hall.

Pratt, D.D. and Collins, J. (2006) Five perspectives on teaching, paper presented at the *International Problem-based Learning Symposium: Reinventing Problem-based Learning*, Singapore (accessed 2 October 2007 at: www.rp.sg/symposium/download/Summary%20Paragraphs.pdf).

Pryor, J. and Crossouard, B. (2007) A socio-cultural theorisation of formative assessment, *Oxford Review of Education*, 1(1): 1–20.

Putnam, R.D. (2000) *Bowling Alone: The Collapse and Revival of American Community*. New York: Simon & Schuster.

Ramondt, L. (2008) Towards the adoption of Massively Multiplayer Education Gaming, in *Proceedings of ReLIVE08 Conference*, Milton Keynes, 20–21 November (available at: www.open.ac.uk/relive08/).

Ramsden, P. (1984) The context of learning, in F. Marton, D. Hounsell and N.J. Entwistle (eds.) *The Experience of Learning*. Edinburgh: Scottish Academic Press.

Ramsden, P. (1992) *Learning to Teach in Higher Education*. London: Routledge.

Rappa, N.A., Yip, D.K.H. and Baey, S.C. (2009) The role of teacher, student and ICT in enhancing student engagement in multiuservirtual environments, *British Journal of Educational Technology*, 40(1): 61–69.

Revans, R.W. (1983) *ABC of Action Learning*. Bromley: Chartwell Bratt.

Reynolds, M., Sclater, M. and Tickner, S. (2004) A critique of participative discourses adopted in networked learning, in *Proceedings of the Networked Learning Conference*, Lancaster (available at: http://www. networkedlearningconference.org.uk/past/nlc2004/proceedings/individual_papers/olsen_et_al.htm).

Rice, C.D. (2004) *Enlightened Universities: Beyond Political Agendas*. Edinburgh: Policy Institute.

Richardson, J.C. and Newby, T. (2006) The role of students' cognitive engagement in online learning, *American Journal of Distance Education*, 20(1): 23–37.

Richter, J. (2007) SL transcript, *Special Speaker Series in Second Life*, 27 March. Eugene, OR: International Society for Technology and Education.

Rieber, L.P., Smith, L. and Noah, D. (1998). The value of serious play, *Educational Technology*, 38(6): 29–37.

Robertson, G., Czerwinski, M. and van Dantzich, M. (1997) Immersion in desktop virtual reality, in *Proceedings of the 10th Annual ACM Symposium on User Interface Software and Technology*. New York: ACM Press.

Rogers, C. (1969) *Freedom to Learn*. Columbus, OH: Merrill.

Rogers, E.M. (1962) *Diffusion of Innovations*. New York: Free Press.

Rust, C., O'Donovan, B. and Price, M. (2005) A social constructivist assessment process model: how the research literature shows us this could be best practice, *Assessment and Evaluation in Higher Education*, 30(3): 233–241.

Saddington, T. (1998) Exploring the roots and branches of experiential learning, *Lifelong Learning in Europe*, 3(3): 133–138.

Salmon, G. (2009) The future for (second) life and learning, *British Journal of Educational Technology*, 40(3): 526–538.

Salmon, G. and Edirisingha, P. (2008) *Podcasting for Learning in Universities*. Maidenhead: McGraw-Hill.

Sambell, K. and McDowell, L. (1998) The construction of the hidden curriculum: messages and meanings in the assessment of student learning, *Assessment and Evaluation in Higher Education*, 23(4): 391–402.

Sambell, K., McDowell, L. and Brown, S. (1997) 'But is it fair?': an exploratory study of student perceptions of the consequential validity of assessment, *Studies in Educational Evaluation*, 23(4): 349–371.

Savin-Baden, M. (2000) *Problem-based Learning in Higher Education: Untold Stories*. Buckingham: Open University Press/SRHE.

Savin-Baden, M. (2006) Disjunction as a form of troublesome knowledge in problem-based learning, in J. Meyer and R. Land (eds.) *Overcoming Barriers to Student Understanding: Threshold Concepts and Troublesome Knowledge*. London: Routledge.

Savin-Baden, M. (2007a) A *Practical Guide to Problem-based Learning Online*. London: Routledge.

Savin-Baden, M. (2008) From cognitive capability to social reform? Shifting perceptions of learning in immersive virtual worlds, *ALT-J: Special issue on Learning in Immersive Virtual Worlds*, 16(3): 151–161.

Savin-Baden, M. (2010) Changelings and shape shifters? Identity play and pedagogical positioning of staff in immersive virtual worlds, *London Review of Education*, 8(1): 25–38.

Savin-Baden, M. and Major, C. (eds.) (2010) *New Approaches to Qualitative Research: Wisdom and Uncertainty*. London: Routledge.

Savin-Baden, M. and Sinclair, C. (2010) Lurking on the threshold: being learners in silent spaces, in R. Land and S. Bayne (eds.) *Digital Differences*. Rotterdam: Sense Publishers.

Savin-Baden, M. and Tombs, C. (2010) Provisionality, play and pluralism in liminal spaces, in R. Sharpe, H. Beetham and S. de Freitas (eds.) *Rethinking Learning for a Digital Age: How Learners are Shaping Their Own Experiences*. London: Routledge.

Savin-Baden, M., Gourlay, L. and Tombs, C. (2010a) Researching in immersive spaces, in M. Savin-Baden and C. Major (eds.) *New Approaches to Qualitative Research: Wisdom and Uncertainty*. London: Routledge.

Savin-Baden, M., Gourlay, L., Mawer, M., Steils, N. and Tombs, G. (2010b) Situating pedagogies, positions and practices in immersive virtual worlds, *Educational Research: Special Issue on Virtual Worlds and Education*, June.

Schoenfeld, A.H. (1989) Exploration of students' mathematical beliefs and behaviour, *Journal for Research in Mathematics Education*, 20: 338–355.

Sharples, M. (2009) Towards an interdisciplinary design science of learning, in D. Cress, V. Dimitrova and M. Specht (eds.) *Learning in the Synergy of Multiple Disciplines*. Lecture Notes in Computer Science #5794. Berlin: Springer.

Sharples, M., Taylor, J. and Vavoula, G. (2005) Towards a theory of mobile learning, paper presented at *mLearn 2005*, Cape Town (accessed 31 October 2006 at: www.mlearn.org.za/CD/papers/Sharples-%20Theory%20of%20Mobile.pdf).

Sibbett, C.H. and Thompson, W.T. (2008) Nettlesome knowledge, liminal-ity and the taboo in cancer and art therapy experiences: implications for learning and teaching, in R. Land, J.H.F. Meyer and J. Smith, J. (eds.) *Threshold Concepts within the Disciplines*. Rotterdam: Sense Publishers.

Slater, M., Perez-Marcos, D., Ehrsson, H.H. and Sanchez-Vives, M.V. (2009) Inducing illusory ownership of a virtual body, *Frontiers in Neuroscience*, 3(2): 214–220.

Slator, B.M., Hill, C. and Del Val, D. (2004) Teaching computer science with virtual worlds, *IEEE Transactions on Education*, 47(2): 269–275.

Steinkuehler, C. (2007) Massively Multiplayer Online Gaming as a con-stellation of literacy practices, *E-Learning*, 4(3): 297–318.

Stellarc (2009) *High Fidelity Illusion* (accessed 22 April 2009 at: http://www.stelarc.va.com.au/highfid/highfid.html).

Steuer, J. (1992) Defining virtual reality: dimensions determining telep-resence, *Journal of Communication*, 42(24): 73–93.

Swales, J. (1990) *Genre Analysis: English in Academic and Research Settings*. Cambridge: Cambridge University Press.

Szita, I., Spronck, P., Ponsen, M. and Sprinkhuzen-Kuyper, I. (2006) Adap-tive game AI with dynamic scripting, *Machine Learning*, 63(3): 217–248.

Talbot, M. (2009) Aaargh! Why are we all here? The philosophy tu-tor's perspective, Open Habitat Magazine, March (available at: http://magazine.openhabitat.org/).

Taylor, R., Barr, J. and Steele, T. (2002) *For a Radical Higher Education after Postmodernism,* Maidenhead: Open University Press/SRHE.

Thackray, L., Good, J. and Howland, K. (2008) Difficult, dangerous, im-possible . . . : crossing the boundaries into immersive virtual worlds, in *Proceedings of ReLIVE08 Conference*, Milton Keynes, 20–21 November (available at: www.open.ac.uk/relive08/).

Trafford, V. (2008) Conceptual frameworks as a threshold concept in doc-torateness, in R. Land, J.H.F Meyer and J. Smith (eds.) *Threshold Concepts within the Disciplines*. Rotterdam: Sense Publishers.

Trigwell, K., Prosser, M. and Waterhouse, F. (1999) Relations between teachers' approaches to teaching and students' approaches to learn-ing, *Higher Education*, 37: 57–70.

Truelove, I. (2009) If we can't build bridges, let's plant trees: the art and de-sign tutor's perspective, *Open Habitat Magazine* (accessed 22 July 2009 at: http://magazine.openhabitat.org/page/open-habitat-magazine).

Truelove, I. and Hibbert, G. (2008) Learning to walk before you know your name: pre-Second Life scaffolding for noobs, in *Proceedings of ReLIVE08 Conference*, Milton Keynes, 20–21 November (available at: www.open.ac.uk/relive08/).

Turkle, S. (1996) *Life on the Screen: Identity in the Age of the Internet*. London: Phoenix.

Turkle, S. (2005) *The Second Self: Computers and the Human Spirit*. Cambridge, MA: MIT Press.

Ulmer, G. (2003a) *Internet Invention: From Literacy to Electracy*. New York: Longman.

Ulmer, G. (2003b) *Web Supplement to Internet Invention: From Literacy to Electracy* (accessed 1 May 2006 at: www.nwe.ufl.edu/~gulmer/longman/pedagogy/).

Vavoula, G.N. and Sharples, M. (2007) Future Technology Workshop: a collaborative method for the design of new learning technologies and activities, *International Journal of Computer Supported Collaborative Learning*, 2(4): 393–419.

Vygotsky, L.S. (1978) *Mind in Society: The Development of Higher Psychological Processes*. Cambridge, MA: Harvard University Press.

Wachowski, L. and Wachowski, A. (2000) *The Art of the Matrix*. New York: Newmarket Press.

Wang, F. and Hannafin, M.J. (2005) Design-based research and technology-enhanced learning environments, *Educational Technology Research and Development*, 53(4): 5–23.

Warburton, S. (2008). Loving your avatar: identity, immersion and empathy, *Liquid Learning* (available at: http://warburton.typepad.com/liquidlearning/2008/01/ loving-your-ava.html).

Warburton, S. (2009). Second Life in higher education: assessing the potential for and the barriers to deploying virtual worlds in learning and teaching, *British Journal of Educational Technology*, 40(3): 414–426.

Weil, S.W. and McGill, I. (eds.) (1989) *Making Sense of Experiential Learning: Diversity in Theory and Practice*. Milton Keynes: Open University Press/SRHE.

Woods, D. (2000) Helping your students gain the most from PBL, in O.S. Tan, P. Little, S.Y. Hee and J. Conway (eds.) *Problem-based Learning: Educational Innovation across Disciplines*. Singapore: Temasek Centre for Problem-Based Learning.

Žižek, S. (1999) The matrix, or two sides of perversion, *Philosophy Today: Supplement on Extending the Horizons of Continental Philosophy*, 43 (available at: http://www.nettime.org/Lists-Archives/nettime-l-9912/msg00019.html).

Žižek, S. (2005) Interrogating the Real. London: Continuum.

# Bibliography

Abraham, R.R., Kamath, A., Upadhya, S. and Ramnarayan, K. (2006) Learning approaches to physiology of undergraduates in an Indian medical school, *Medical Education*, 40: 916–923.

Abraham, R.R., Vinod, P., Kamath, M.G., Asha, K. and Ramnarayan, K. (2008) Learning approaches of undergraduate medical students to physiology in a non-PBL- and partially PBL-oriented curriculum, *Advances in Physiology Education*, 32: 35–37.

Barnett, R. (2003) *Beyond all Reason: Living with Ideology in the University*. Buckingham: Open University Press/SRHE.

Bayne, S. (2005) Deceit, desire and control: the identities of learners and teachers in cyberspace, in R. Land and S. Bayne (eds.) *Education in Cyberspace*. London: Routledge.

Beetham, H. and Sharpe, R. (eds.) (2007) *Rethinking Pedagogy for the Digital Age: Designing and Delivering E-Learning*. London: RoutledgeFalmer.

Belenky, M.F., Clinchy, B.M., Goldberger, N.R. and Tarule, J.M. (1986) *Women's Ways of Knowing*. New York: Basic Books.

Bell, V., Grech, E., Maiden, C., Halligan, P.W. and Ellis, H.D. (2005) 'Internet delusions': a case series and theoretical integration, *Psychopathology*, 38: 144–150.

Bergin, R. and Fors, U. (2003) Interactive simulation of patients – an advanced tool for student-activated learning in medicine and healthcare, *Computers and Education*, 40(4): 361–376.

Biggs, J. (1999) *Teaching for Quality Learning at University*. Buckingham: Open University Press/SRHE.

Birenbaum, M. (1995) Assessment 2000: towards a pluralistic approach to assessment, in M. Birenbaum and F.J.R.C. Dochy (eds.) *Alternatives in Assessment of Achievements, Learning Processes and Prior Knowledge*. Boston, MA: Kluwer Academic.

Birenbaum, M., Breuer, K., Cascallar, E., Dochy, F., Dorie, Y., Ridgway, J. et al. (2006) A learning integrated assessment system, *Educational Research Review*, 1(1): 61–67.

Boud, D. (2000) Sustainable assessment: rethinking assessment for the learning society, *Studies in Continuing Education*, 22(2): 151–167.

Boud, D. and Falchikov, N. (2006) Aligning assessment with long-term learning, *Assessment and Evaluation in Higher Education*, 41(4): 399–413.

Boud, D., Cohen, R. and Sampson, J. (eds.) (2001) *Peer Learning in Higher Education: Learning With and From Each Other.* London: Kogan Page.

Bovill, C., Aitken, G., Hutchison, J., Morrison, F., Roseweir, K., Scott, A. et al. (2010) Experiences of learning through collaborative evaluation from a Masters Programme in Professional Education, *International Journal for Academic Development*, 15(2): 143–154.

Brownell, J. and Jameson, D.A. (2004) Problem-based learning in graduate management education: an integrative model and interdisciplinary application, *Journal of Management Education*, 28: 558–577.

Bruner, J. (1966) *Toward a Theory of Instruction.* Cambridge, MA: Harvard University Press.

Carlson, L. (1989) Effective moderation of computer conferences: hints for moderators, in M.G. Brochet (ed.) *Moderating Conferences.* Guelph, Ontario: University of Guelph.

Caruso, D.R. and Salovey, P. (2004) *The Emotionally Intelligent Manager: How to Develop and Use the Four Emotional Skills of Leadership.* San Francisco, CA: Jossey-Bass.

Collis, B. (1997) Pedagogical reengineering: a pedagogical approach to course enrichment and redesign with the WWW, *Educational Technology Review*, 8: 11–15.

Conole, G., de Laat, M., Dillon, T. and Darby, T. (2006) *JISC LXP Student Experiences of Technologies – Final Report*, November 2006. Bristol: JISC.

Cousin, G. (2005) Learning from cyberspace, in R. Land and S. Bayne (eds.) *Education in Cyberspace.* Abingdon: RoutledgeFalmer.

Delanty, G. (2001) *Challenging Knowledge: The University in the Knowledge Society.* Buckingham: Open University Press/SRHE.

Dennerlein, J., Becker, T., Johnson, P., Reynolds, C. and Picard, R.W. (2003) Frustrating computers users increases exposure to physical factors, in *Proceedings of the International Ergonomics Association*, Seoul, Korea, 24–29 August.

Denzin, N. (1989) *Interpretive Interactionism.* London: Sage.

Entwistle, N.J. (1981) *Styles of Learning and Teaching.* New York: Wiley.

Evans, P. (2009) Is there a link between problem-based learning and emotional intelligence?, *Kathmandu University Medical Journal*, 7(1): 4–7.

Garrison, D.R. and Kanuka, H. (2004) Blended learning: uncovering its transformative potential in higher education, *The Internet and Higher Education*, 7(2): 95–105.

Gibbs, G. and Simpson, C. (2005) Conditions under which assessment supports learning, *Learning and Teaching in Higher Education*, 1(1): 3–31.

Giroux, H.A. and Giroux, S. (2004) *Take Back Higher Education.* London: Palgrave.

Goffman, E. (1963) *Stigma: Notes on the Management of Spoiled Identity*. New York: Prentice-Hall.

Goleman, D. (1995) *Emotional Intelligence*. New York: Bantam Books.

Habermas, J. (1984) *The Theory of Communicative Action*, Vol. 1. Cambridge: Polity.

Hämäläinen, R., Manninen, T., Järvelä, S. and Häkkinen, P. (2006) Learning to collaborate: designing collaboration in a 3-D game environment, *The Internet and Higher Education*, 9(1): 47–61.

Haraway, D. (1991) *Simians, Cyborgs, and Women: The Reinvention of Nature*. London: Routledge.

Heron, J. (1988) Assessment revisited, in D. Boud (ed.) *Developing Student Autonomy in Learning*. London: Kogan Page.

Hoey, M. (2005) *Lexical Priming: A New Theory of Words and Language*. Abingdon: Routledge.

Hoey, M. (2006) Language as choice: what is chosen?, in S. Hunston and G. Thompson (eds.) *System and Corpus: Exploring Connections*. London: Equinox.

Jacobsen, D.Y. (1997) *Tutorial processes in a problem-based learning context: medical students' reception and negotiations*. Unpublished PhD thesis, Norwegian University of Science and Technology, Trondheim.

Jung, K. (1977) *The Symbolic Life: Miscellaneous Writings. The Collected Works of C.G. Jung*, Vol. 18. Princeton, NJ: Princeton University Press.

Kane, P. (2005) *The Play Ethic: A Manifesto for a Different Way of Living*. London: Pan.

Kang, M., Kim, S., Choi, H. and Park, S. (2007) Validating an Emotional Presence Scale to measure online learners' engagement, in T. Bastiaens and S. Carliner (eds.) *Proceedings of World Conference on E-Learning in Corporate, Government, Healthcare, and Higher Education 2007*. Chesapeake, VA: AACE.

Knight, P. (2002) Summative assessment in higher education: practices in disarray, *Studies in Higher Education*, 27(3): 277–286.

Knight, P. and Yorke, M. (2004) *Learning, Curriculum and Employability in Higher Education*. London: Routledge.

Knight, P.T. (2000) The value of a programme-wide approach to assessment, *Assessment and Evaluation in Higher Education*, 25(3): 237–251.

LaGravenese, R. (1995) Bridges of Madison County, the (1995) movie script based on a novel by Waller, R.J. (1992) *The Bridges of Madison County*. New York: Warner Books Inc.

Langdon, R. and Coltheart, M. (2000) The cognitive neuropsychology of delusions, in M. Coltheart and M. Davies (eds.) *Pathologies of Belief*. Oxford: Blackwell.

Lillis, T. and Turner, J. (2002) Student writing in higher education: contemporary confusion, traditional concerns, *Teaching in Higher Education*, 6(1): 57–68.

Livingstone, D. and Kemp, J. (2008) Mixed-methods and mixed-worlds: engaging globally distributed user groups for extended evaluation studies, in *Proceedings of ReLIVE08 Conference*, Milton Keynes, 20–21 November (available at: www.open.ac.uk/relive08/).

Marshall, J. and Halligan, P. (1996) Introduction, in P. Halligan and J. Marshall (eds.) *Method in Madness*. Hove: Psychology Press.

Mason, H. and Moutahir, M. (2006) Multidisciplinary experiential education in Second Life: a global approach, in D. Livingstone and J. Kemp (eds.) *Proceedings of the Second Life Education Workshop*. Paisley: University of Paisley (available at: http://www.simteach.com/SLCC06/).

Miller, C., Veletsianos, G. and Hooper, S. (2006) Demystifying aesthetics: an exploration of emotional design, in *The Ninth IASTED International Conference on Computers and Advanced Technology in Education*, Lima, Peru, 4–6 October.

Minocha, S. and Tingle, R. (2008) Socialisation and collaborative learning of distance learners in 3-D virtual worlds, in *Proceedings of ReLIVE08 Conference*, Milton Keynes, 20–21 November (available at: www.open.ac.uk/relive08/).

Nicol, D. and Macfarlane-Dick, D. (2006) Formative assessment and self-regulated learning: a model and seven principles of good feedback practice, *Studies in Higher Education*, 31(2): 199–218.

O'Donovan, B., Price, M. and Rust, C. (2008) Developing student understanding of assessment standards: a nested hierarchy of approaches, *Teaching in Higher Education*, 13(2): 205–217.

Oliver, R. and Herrington, J. (2003) Exploring technology-mediated learning from a pedagogical perspective, *Journal of Interactive Learning Environments*, 11(2): 111–126.

Parker, J. (2002) A new disciplinarity: communities of knowledge, learning and practice, *Teaching in Higher Education: Special Issue on Disciplinary Pedagogy*, 7(4): 373–386.

Pekrun, R., Goetz, T., Titz, W. and Perry, R. (2002) Academic emotions in students' self-regulated learning and achievement: a program of qualitative and quantitative research, *Educational Psychologist*, 37(2): 91–105.

Perry, C. and Ball, I. (2005) Emotional intelligence and teaching: further validation evidence, *Issues in Educational Research*, 15 (available at: http://www.iier.org.au/iier15/perry.html).

Perry, W.G. (1970) *Forms of Intellectual and Ethical Development During the College Years: A Scheme*. New York: Holt, Rinehart & Winston.

Peters, O. (1998) *Learning and Teaching in Distance Education: Pedagogical Analyses and Interpretations in an International Perspective*. London: Kogan Page.

Pratt, D.D. and Associates (1998) *Five Perspectives on Teaching in Adult and Higher Education*. Malabar, FL: Krieger Publishers.

Price, M. and Rust, C. (1999) The experience of introducing a common criteria assessment grid across an academic department, *Quality in Higher Education*, 5(2): 133–144.

Price, M., O'Donovan, B. and Rust, C. (2007) Putting a social-constructivist assessment process model into practice: building the feedback loop into the assessment process through peer-feedback, *Innovations in Education and Teaching International*, 44(2): 143–152.

Ratner, C. (2000) A cultural-psychological analysis of emotions, *Culture and Psychology*, 2(6): 5–39.

Rayner, K. (1998) Eye movements in reading and information processing: 20 years of research, *Psychological Bulletin*, 124(3): 372–422.

Reeves, T. (2002) Storm clouds on the digital education horizon, in A. Williamson, C. Gunn, A. Young and T. Clear (eds.) *Winds of Change in the Sea of Learning: Proceedings of the 19th Annual Conference of the Australasian Society for Computers in Learning in Tertiary Education*. Auckland, NZ: UNITEC Institute of Technology.

Rieber, L.P. (1996) Seriously considering play: designing interactive learning environments based on the blending of microworlds, simulations, and games, *Educational Technology Research and Development*, 44(2): 43–58.

Rosenau, P.M. (1992) *Post-Modernism and the Social Sciences: Insights, Inroads, and Intrusions*. Princeton, NJ: Princeton University Press.

Rust, C., Price, M. and O'Donovan, B. (2003) Improving students' learning by developing their understanding of assessment criteria and processes, *Assessment and Evaluation in Higher Education*, 28(2): 147–164.

Sadler, D.R. (1989) Formative assessment and the design of instructional systems, *Instructional Science*, 18: 119–144.

Salmon, G. (2003) *E-Moderating: The Key to Teaching and Learning Online*. London: Kogan Page.

Salovey. P. and Mayer, J.D. (1990) Emotional intelligence, *Imagination, Cognition and Personality*, 9: 185–211.

Savin-Baden, M. (2007b) *Learning Spaces: Creating Opportunities for Knowledge Creation in Academic Life*. Maidenhead: McGraw-Hill.

Savin-Baden, M., Tombs, C., White, D., Kavia, S., Poulton, T. and Woodham, L. (2009) *Getting Started with Second Life*. Bristol: JISC (available at: http://www.jisc.ac.uk/publications/documents/gettingstartedsecond life.aspx).

Scalese, R.J., Obeso, V.T. and Issenberg, S.B. (2008) Simulation technology for skills training and competency assessment in medical education, *Journal of General Internal Medicine, Supplement*, 23(1): 46–49.

Seymour, W. (2001) In the flesh or online? Exploring qualitative research methodologies, *Qualitative Research*, 1(2): 147–168.

Shakespeare, W. (1590/2002) A Midsummer Night's Dream, in *The Complete Pelican Shakespeare*. London: Penguin

Sharpe, R., Benfield, G., Lessner, E. and DeCicco, E. (2005) *Learner Scoping Study: Final Report* (accessed 19 November 2007 at: www.jisc.ac.uk/index.cfm?name=elp_learneroutcomes).

Shen, L., Wang, M. and Shen, R. (2009) Affective e-learning: using 'emotional' data to improve learning in pervasive learning environment, *Educational Technology and Society*, 12(2): 176–189.

Sherwood, C. (1991) Adventure games in the classroom: a far cry from A says Apple ..., *Computers and Education*, 17(4): 309–315.

Slater, M. (2009) Place illusion and plausibility can lead to realistic behaviour in immersive virtual environments, *Philosophical Transactions of the Royal Society of London: Series B, Biological Sciences*, 364(1535): 3549–3557.

Slater, M. and Wilbur, S. (1997) A framework for immersive virtual environments (FIVE): speculations on the role of presence in virtual environments, *Presence: Teleoperators and Virtual Environments*, 6(6): 603–616.

Slator, B.M., Hill, C. and Del Val, D. (2004) Teaching computer science with virtual worlds, *IEEE Transactions on Education*, 47(2): 269–275.

Stenhouse, L. (1975) *An Introduction to Curriculum Research and Development*. London: Heinemann.

Trinder, K. (2008) Fearing your avatar? Exploring the scary journey to the 3rd dimension, in *Proceedings of ReLIVE08 Conference*, Milton Keynes, 20–21 November (available at: www.open.ac.uk/relive08/).

Usher, R. and Edwards, R. (1994) *Postmodernism and Education*. London: Routledge.

Warburton, S. (2008) *How Tall is Tall in Second Life?* (accessed 9 March 2009 at: http://warburton.typepad.com/liquidlearning/2008/06/how-tall-is-tal.html).

Wiederhold, B.K., Gevirtz, R. and Wiederhold, M.D. (1998) Fear of flying: a case report using virtual reality therapy with physiological monitoring, *CyberPsychology and Behavior*, 1(2): 97–103.

Yee, N. (2009) The demographics and derived experiences of users of massively multi-user online graphical environments, paper presented at the *Annual Meeting of the International Communication Association*, New York (available at: http://www.allacademic.com/meta/p13958_index.html).

Žižek, S. (1998) *The Cyberspace Real World*, Association of Psychoanalysis (available at: www.wapol.org).

# Index

**CHALLENGING E-LEARNING IN THE UNIVERSITY**

Robin Goodfellow and Mary R. Lea

9780335220878 (Paperback)
2007

eBook also available

*Challenging e-learning in the University* takes a new approach to the growing field of e-learning in higher education. In it, the authors argue that in order to develop e-learning in the university we need to understand the texts and practices that are involved in learning and teaching using online and web-based technologies.

**Key features:**

- Provides an alternative perspective to the 'how to do it' books on e-learning
- It develops an approach which draws together social and cultural approaches to literacies, learning and technologies
- Uses case studies to explore approaches to practices covered

www.openup.co.uk

**OPEN UNIVERSITY PRESS**
McGraw - Hill Education

## PODCASTING FOR LEARNING IN UNIVERSITIES

Gilly Salmon and Palitha Edirisingha

9780335234295 (Paperback)
2008

eBook also available

*Podcasting for Learning in Universities* details several examples of research to practice for the successful use of podcasts in Higher Education, drawing from studies in the UK, Australia and South Africa. The book offers a practical transferable model and guidelines for integrating podcasts in higher education contexts.

**Key features:**

- Dedicated website at **www.podcastingforlearning.com** with further links and examples
- Case studies covering areas such as reflective learning, active learning
- 10-step pedagogic model for developing podcasting effectively

www.openup.co.uk